TWAYNE'S WORLD AUTHORS SERIES
A Survey of the World's Literature

CHINA

William Schultz, University of Arizona

EDITOR

Wu Ching-tzu

TWAS 495

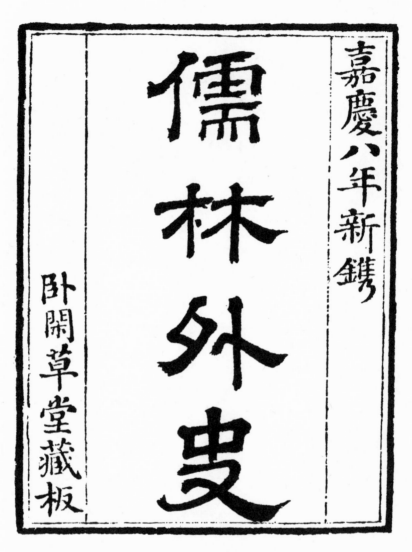

嘉慶八年新鐫

儒林外史

卧閑草堂藏板

The title page from the 1803 Wo-hsien ts'ao-t'ang edition of the
Ju-lin wai-shih, the earliest of many extant editions; taken from the
1975 photolithographic edition of the Jen-min wen-hsüeh ch'u-pan
she in Peking.

WU CHING-TZU

By TIMOTHY C. WONG

Arizona State University

TWAYNE PUBLISHERS

A DIVISION OF G. K. HALL & CO., BOSTON

845.13
W959 W
1978

Library of Congress Cataloging in Publication Data

Wong, Timothy C
  Wu Ching-tzu.

  (Twayne's world authors series ; TWAS 495)
  Revision of the author's thesis, Stanford University.
  Bibliography: p. 151–58
  Includes index.
  1. Wu, Ching-tzu, 1701–1754. Ju lin wai shih.
  2. Wu, Ching-tzu, 1701–1754—Criticism and interpretation.
PL2732.U22J889   1978   895.1'3'4   78-2692
ISBN 0-8057-6336-8

To the Memory of My Mother

Contents

About the Author

Timothy C. Wong is an Assistant Professor of Chinese at Arizona State University where he has been teaching since 1974. He was born in Hong Kong and raised in Honolulu, Hawaii. He received his B.A. in Political Science from Saint Mary's College in California in 1963; his M.A. in Asian Studies from the University of Hawaii in 1968, where he was an East-West Center grantee; and his Ph.D. in Chinese from Stanford University in 1975. He has also studied at the Inter-University Program for Chinese Language Studies in Taipei and the Inter-University Program for Japanese Language Studies in Tokyo. Professor Wong has previously authored articles and reviews in such journals as *Literature East and West, The Journal of Oriental Literature*, and the *Journal of the American Oriental Society*.

Preface

Judging from the many nineteenth- and early twentieth-century editions, extant and referred to, of Wu Ching-tzu's satirical novel *Ju-lin wai-shih*, we can surmise that the work enjoyed a certain popularity for many decades. Literary historians, moreover, list it regularly in the company of the *Romance of the Three Kingdoms* (*San-kuo yen-yi*), *Water Margin* (*Shui-hu chüan*), *Journey to the West* (*Hsi-yu chi*), *Golden Lotus* (*Chin P'ing Mei*), and the *Red Chamber Dream* (*Hung-lou meng*) as one of the six greatest novels of traditional China. And yet the contemporary scholar Hu Shih is certainly right when he wrote that "among first class novels, the circulation of the *Ju-lin wai-shih* is the least broad"; and the modern writer Lu Hsün's wry comment that, in recent years, the *Ju-lin wai-shih* is "no longer great," because "to be great, someone has to understand it," constitutes a point well taken.

While much of Chinese fiction has posed problems for critics— since it is now difficult, perhaps impossible, to consider traditional Chinese works on their own terms—interpretations of the *Ju-lin wai-shih* which have emerged in recent years show that it is probably the most misunderstood of the major Chinese novels. The problem is both general and particular. Generally speaking, much of Chinese fictional art appears to emanate from premises different from those of its modern, Western counterpart, and thus it challenges its critics to constantly retest and reevaluate literary principles assumed to be universal; this challenge can be exciting, but its demands on critics can sometimes prove overwhelming. In regard to the *Ju-lin wai-shih* itself, moreover, the tendency has been to group it together with fictional works of a vastly different nature, thus largely ignoring its satirical character in the evaluation of its art.

This book, therefore, attempts, like other recent studies of Chinese fiction, to account for cultural and literary factors. It considers the *Ju-lin wai-shih* as a work in the Chinese tradition, and it will discuss this work as satire, taking into consideration satire's rhetorical and didactic nature. The particular conclusions it comes to are really of secondary importance; they are intended to stimulate discussion along more precise lines rather than to be taken as final and incontrovertible. A book of this sort inevitably begins its journey to obsolescence from the moment of its completion. If, along the way, it can help stimulate ideas and discoveries which add to our still elementary knowledge of traditional Chinese fiction as a whole, then the effort I have made in putting it together will not have been in vain.

My work on Wu Ching-tzu and his novel spans a number of years and has benefitted from the kindnesses of many. I would especially like to thank Professors John C. Y. Wang, James J. Y. Liu, and William Lyell of Stanford University; Professor William R. Schultz of the University of Arizona; Professor Paul S. Ropp of Memphis State University; and Mrs. Eugenia Y. Tu of Arizona State University. Finally, I should mention my wife Elizabeth who, throughout this past summer, bore the brunt of caring for a colicky infant as I went off daily to my typewriter.

A generous fellowship from the Giles Whiting Foundation in 1973–1974 first enabled me to set down my research and my ideas in a Ph.D. dissertation for Stanford University. Subsequently, I was able to revise this dissertation in successive summers, owing to a Faculty Grant-in-Aid from Arizona State University and a Grant-in-Aid for Recent Receipients of the Ph.D. from the American Council of Learned Societies. I am deeply grateful to all these organizations. Also, I am indebted to the Center for Asian Studies, Arizona State University, for its assistance.

In general, I have followed the Wade-Giles system of romanization of all Chinese names, words, and titles in this study (omitting the meaningless circumflex and using *yi* for *i* for those unfamiliar with the Chinese language), even though I am well aware that many publications on Chinese subjects have now changed over to the *pinyin* system. The reason for this is pragmatic: the available English version of the *Ju-lin wai-shih*, translated as the *Scholars* by Yang Hsien-yi and Gladys Yang, uses a modified Wade-Giles system (discarding the umlaut and the apostrophe from the standard), and, for readers without knowledge of Chinese who would want to refer to the English text, my use of another system of romanization would constitute an unnecessary barrier. To facilitate such reference, in fact, I have deliberately adhered to the Yangs' transliteration or translation of all names of the novel's characters, giving, whenever a difference occurs, the standard Wade-Giles transcription in parentheses the first time such a name is mentioned.

Preface

The many quotations from the text of the novel follow the Yang's translation, except in places where I regard the rendering as unfaithful to the original or where a different wording would better bring out whatever point I am making at the time. All other translations, unless otherwise noted, are my own.

The best known place names (Nanking, Peking, Yangtze) are given in the commonly used "post office" spelling; all others appear in standard Wade-Giles even though, in some cases, the "post office" version is initially given in parentheses; for example, Yang-chou (Yangchow).

I have chosen to refer to Wu Ching-tzu's novel in transliterated form because the title *The Scholars*, by which it is known in English, is so far removed from the original as to make me uncomfortable. A satisfactory translation, on the other hand, would be too long and cumbersome to cite as often as I have had to in this study. I hope the reader will forgive me this little idiocyncrasy.

TIMOTHY C. WONG

Arizona State University

Acknowledgments

Chapter 5 of this book has been previously published as "Rhetorical Realism: Psychological Descriptions in the *Ru-lin wai-shi*," in *Selected Papers in Asian Studies*, Western Conference of the Association for Asian Studies, vol. 1 (Albuquerque, 1976). I am grateful to the conference for permission to reprint the article in revised form.

Chronology

1701   Wu Ching-tzu born, probably in Ch'üan-chiao, Anhwei Province.

1713   Death of his mother.

1714   Follows his father Wu Lin-ch'i to Kan-yü County in Chiang-su (Kiangsu) Province, where the latter assumes a minor official post.

1723   Obtains *sheng-yüan* (or *hsiu-ts'ai*) degree in civil service examinations. Death of his father. Begins life of dissipation.

1728   Death of first wife, née T'ao.

1729   Continues taking *sui* and *k'o* examinations for *sheng-yuan* in Ch'u-chou.

1733   Moves permanently to Nanking; withdraws from further participation in examinations and begins eremitic life.

1736   Recommended for *Po-hsüeh hung-tz'u* ("Great Literary Scholarship") examination; declines ostensibly because of poor health. Begins the *Ju-lin wai-shih*(?).

1743(?) Takes part in sacrificial rituals to Ts'ang Chieh on Rain Flower Terrace (Yü-ha T'ai) in Nanking.

1748–   *Ju-lin wai-shih* completed or largely completed.
1750

1754   Wu Ching-tzu dies suddenly on December 11, while visiting friends in Yang-chou (Yangchow).

1768–   *Ju-lin wai-shih* first published in Yang-chou by Chin Chao-
1779   yen.

CHAPTER 1

The Evolution of a Satirist

WU Ching-tzu lived out his years in eighteenth-century China, a time when persons of his patrician background and upbringing engaged themselves in a variety of leisurely pursuits. Accordingly, during his not uneventful life, Wu was a poet, a classicist, a calligrapher, an historiographer, an essayist, and, by his own account, a composer of some distinction among the dramatists in the gay quarters of his beloved Nanking.[1] And it was probably during the last decade and a half of his life that he wrote the *Ju-lin wai-shih* ("Unofficial History of the Literati," since translated as *The Scholars*), a work of satirical fiction in the vernacular language.

Although by Wu's time Chinese fiction—*hsiao-shuo*, or the insignificant gossip of the alleyways and the market places—had had some staunch defenders, it was still a long way from being regarded as the proper business of a man of letters.[2] We have no record of what Wu thought of his own venture into *hsiao-shuo* writing, but it is likely that he would have preferred to be remembered for his more orthodox endeavors. Yet even during his own lifetime his poetry and his scholarship were so eclipsed by his skill at fiction that a friend was moved to write the following lines:

> The *Unofficial History* records the literati:
> How charmingly, skillfully hewn!
> Still I grieve for this man
> Who must by fiction be known.[3]

These words also proved to be prophetic. Today, except for a slim volume of his poetry, only the *Ju-lin wai-shih* remains to give testimony to his worth as an author. But even if the entire corpus of his other writings would, by some miracle, be recovered, it would not likely give him a higher place in the history of Chinese literature

15

than the one he now occupies as the pioneer of Chinese fiction in the satirical mode. The following account of his life, therefore, is not directed toward an examination of Wu's growth, maturity, and decline as a man; rather, it will subordinate all that is known about him to a consideration of him as a satirist, for it is as a satirist that he is rightfully accorded a high place in the history of Chinese literature.

In talking of a man "as a satirist," there is always the temptation to trace in his life patterns or characteristics common to satirists as a group.[4] To do this with Wu Ching-tzu would be interesting but probably neither valid nor instructive. For while common patterns can undoubtedly be found between Wu and those satirists familiar to a Western reader, it is far more important to our ultimate understanding of the man to consider him apart from preconceived or predelineated notions. On the other hand, this study will be speculative in attempting to link Wu Ching-tzu's character, background, and cultural outlook to the analysis of his satire. As I shall explain in a later chapter, Wu's satire is topical enough to demand in its explanation an explication of the circumstances to which it refers. The facts of Wu's life and times have a more direct relevance to the *Ju-lin wai-shih* than, for example, those of a poet's life to his lyric poetry.

I *Wu Ching-tzu's Forebears*

A central fact of Wu Ching-tzu's life is the high achievements and fame of his forebears, a fact which was to him at once a source of unceasing pride and, contrasted with his own failures in life, an eventual psychological burden. It is, therefore, not unreasonable to conclude that the satire he wrote was also an apology for his inability to match the success so common in his family over four previous generations.

Some time during the Ming dynasty (1368–1644), Wu Ching-tzu's ancestors settled in Ch'üan-chiao (Chuantsiao) in the province of Anhwei, in the thickly populated, fertile, and cultured Yangtze Plain of southeastern China where Wu was to spend his entire life. As farmers and then as physicians, they moved up the ladder of success, like all Chinese of the time, by taking the examination route to officialdom. Wu's great great-grandfather Wu P'ei began the process in the latter part of the Ming dynasty by becoming a *lin-sheng*, or student on government stipend.[5] Wu P'ei fathered five sons, four of whom far surpassed him by becoming *chin-shih* (metropolitan graduates), thus attaining the highest degree possible. Among them Wu Kuo-tui (1616–1680), Wu Ching-tzu's great-grandfather, who received this ultimate degree under the new Ch'ing dynasty (1644–1911), was the most successful, inasmuch as he finished third in the palace examination of 1658. He subsequently entered the prestigious Han-lin Academy, the highest literary institution in the land, where he advanced from compiler *(pien-hsiu)* to reader *(shih-tu)*.[6] Kuo-tui's son Wu Tan, Wu Ching-tzu's grandfather, is noted in the local histories as a filial son; his success in the civil service examinations was limited, although he did secure a lower degree by purchase and held a minor official post. A brother, however, did become a *chü-jen* ("provincial graduate") and two cousins maintained the family's lofty reputation by becoming *chin-shih* during the reign of the K'ang-hsi emperor. Wu Tan died young, leaving behind a son, Wu Lin-ch'i, a student and minor official of little distinction who became Wu Ching-tzu's father.

Nowhere is Wu Ching-tzu's essential Confucianism more apparent than in the overflowing pride with which he regarded his ancestors, who were largely successful, and the worshipful excesses with which he described his father, who was not. Among his extant poetry is the "Yi-chia *fu*" ("Rhapsody on Moving My Home"), a long piece complete with a preface written in 1733 on the occasion of his leaving his ancestral home in Ch'üan-chiao to reside permanently in Nanking. In what was a sad and bitter hour, he drew courage and comfort from recalling the former glories of his family:

> For fifty years my family flourished:
> As if Chi and Yün of the Lu's were under one roof,
> And Shih and Ch'e of the Su's again dwelt together.[7]
> Sons there were whose talents matched their fathers';
> And before our gates we could boast of the leavings of horses. . . .
> Guests came in carriages of vermillion;
> Maids served with embroidered vests and painted cheeks.
> Our fields glowed with a thousand *mou* of colorful crops;[8]
> Our orchards sparkled with the citrus of a thousand trees. . . .[9]

Born to all of this splendor, Wu Lin-ch'i, as his son tells it, soon became disenchanted with luxury and status and directed his energies toward self-cultivation and the practice of morality. His lack of achievement in the practical world was, in the eyes of his adoring

son, the very index of his higher virtue. "My father," Wu Ching-tzu
wrote in the "Yi-chia *fu*,"

> Distilled the essence of a thousand ages and
> The breadth and width of a hundred generations.
> He was the paragon of the universe,
> Having grasped the writings of the ancient worthies.[10]

Whether Wu Lin-ch'i was actually a man of such wisdom and
virtue is unimportant for our purposes. What *is* important is that
Wu Ching-tzu, probably from an early age, thought that he was.
For, as we shall later see, the idea that worldly success was directly
antithetical to true learning and true virtue became the moral cornerstone of the satirical novel Wu Ching-tzu was to write many
years after his father's death.

II *Wu Ching-tzu's Early Life*

Most of the known facts about Wu Ching-tzu have been uncovered through the personal effort of Hu Shih (1891–1962) and the
collective effort of scholars in the People's Republic of China in the
decade or so after 1954, the bicentennial of Wu Ching-tzu's death. It
was Hu Shih, a pioneer in the modern study of traditional Chinese
fiction, who first provided indisputable proof of Wu Ching-tzu's
authorship of the *Ju-lin wai-shih* and who, with the help of the
Tai-ching T'ang Bookstore in Peking, secured a copy of the *Wen-mu
shan-fang chi*, which contains in four *chüan* the bulk of Wu Ching-
tzu's extant poetry along with two *chüan* of poems by Wu's eldest
son Wu Lang and informative prefaces by seven of Wu's contemporaries.[11] Largely based on this material, Hu Shih in 1922 produced the "Wu Ching-tzu nien-p'u," a detailed chronology of Wu's
life and work which remains the major source of information on the
subject.[12] Since 1954 a succession of articles and one important book
from the People's Republic of China have presented various newly
discovered materials and have modified some of Hu Shih's conclusions; but, over a half century later, many of his findings remain
valid.

Nearly all of Wu Ching-tzu's modern biographers tend to supplement their sources with passages from his fiction. This is really
unnecessary since enough factual sources exist, in the form of his
own poetry and prefaces and the writings of his relatives and ac-

quaintances, to form a fairly detailed outline of his life. These sources have established that Wu was also known by the *tzu* ("courtesy name") of Min-hsüan, as well as the various *hao* ("style names") of Li-min ("a rice-consuming citizen"), Ch'in-huai yü-k'o ("a traveler residing at the Ch'in-huai River [in Nanking]") and Wen-mu lao-jen ("the old man of Wen-mu," after a residence in Ch'uan-chiao called the Wen-mu shan-fang, "the mountain retreat of literary trees").[13] His life spanned the years between 1701 and 1754 which, remarkably, coincide with what has been called the age of satire in the history of English literature. At Wu Ching-tzu's birth, John Dryden had been dead one year; Alexander Pope was a child of thirteen; Joseph Addison and Richard Steele were both twenty-nine; and Jonathan Swift, at thirty-four, had not yet begun to produce his greatest works. Henry Fielding would be born in another six years, and Samuel Johnson in another eight. The turmoil of the political struggle between the Cavaliers and the Puritans which stimulated the satirical style in England did not, however, have its counterpart in China. Wu lived during all or part of the reigns of the K'ang-hsi (1662–1723), Yung-cheng (1723–1736), and Ch'ien-lung (1736–1796), emperors in the Manchu Ch'ing dynasty, a period which, to most historians, represents with whatever weaknesses the high-water mark of the dynasty's achievements of unity, stability, peace, and prosperity.[14] Thus, while there may be some validity in the Marxist attribution of Wu's satire to his historical perceptions of the evils of "feudalism," it is more enlightening in this case to trace his motivations to his personal character and to the particular circumstances of his life.

Little is known about Wu Ching-tzu's childhood. He seems to have been the only natural child of his parents, though he did have an adopted sister of whom he was very fond.[15] In a poem written years later, Wu tells us that his mother died when he was only twelve (or thirteen, by Chinese count). According to his cousin Chin Chü (b. 1684), Wu Ching-tzu at this age was a serious and studious child, attending school in his white mourning garb, and seeking "to penetrate the secret essence of literature and history." He was also a solitary child, refusing to "sport about with the other children,/But retiring to your room like a monk to his cell."[16] Wu Lin-ch'i, possibly because of the premature death of Wu Ching-tzu's mother, devoted much personal attention to the education of this bright, introverted son, seeing to it that he was thoroughly grounded in the

Confucian classics which, to the Chinese of the time, were the
repository of both human reason and human morality.[17] And just as
Wu Ching-tzu revered his father all his life, he never afterward
completely abandoned fundamental Confucian ideals, not even, as
we shall see, in his satirical novel which openly ridiculed those in
service to the state.

Around 1714, when Wu Ching-tzu was just thirteen years old,
Wu Lin-ch'i accepted a minor official post as director of studies
(*chiao-yü*) in Kan-yü *hsien* in the northeastern part of Ching-su
(Kiangsu) province along the seacoast.[18] From that time until 1722,
when Wu Lin-ch'i resigned his post to return to Ch'uan-chiao, Wu
Ching-tzu solidified his knowledge of the classics and history and,
under the careful instruction of a special tutor, grew into a young
man of talent and promise. He could, in the words of his cousin Wu
Ch'ing, "Weave smoothly together, with a sweep of his pen, a composition of a thousand words/Covering the breadth and width of his
subject like silkworms munching leaves of the mulberry."[19] Wu
Ch'ing and others have also given testimony to Wu Ching-tzu's
mastery of rhetoric and of the intricate rules of prosody and rhyme.
At this time, therefore, Wu Ching-tzu appeared a likely prospect to
match the achievements of his ancestors by securing for himself an
examination degree and a post in the government bureaucracy, thus
fulfilling the conventional Confucian injunction to render active service to society. But this was not to be.

From about 1722 his fortunes began to take a downward turn. We
do not really know the cause of his father's resignation from office,
but we do know that his father was seriously ill on returning home.
It was thus with a heavy heart that Wu Ching-tzu, on the old man's
orders, took the examination for the *sheng-yüan* ("government student") degree in 1723. As Chin Liang-ming, another relative, recalls
it, "You hurried back in panic to attend to your dad/Not bothering to
reconsider the good or the bad of your composition." Wu passed,
but what would have been an occasion for joy became instead one of
sorrow, brought about by his father's death. "Before a dark scholar's
gown can adorn your happy smiles," Chin writes, "Your hempen
garments were like snow, your hair in disarray."[20]

There is no record of Wu Ching-tzu's actual feelings at this time,
but the need to leave an ailing father in order to seek public honor
must have had a profound effect. Moreover, the coincidental gain-
ing of a degree with the nearly simultaneous loss of a revered parent

could only have reminded Wu of the age-old conflict between the Confucian obligation to serve the state and the equally Confucian injunction to serve one's parents. Later, as we examine the moral thought of the *Ju-lin wai-shih*, we shall see that this conflict is prominently represented in such characters as Kuang Chao-jen (K'uang Ch'ao-jen) whose worldly ambitions stand in the way of their filiality and who thus become recipients of Wu's satirical barbs.

III   A Troubled Youth

The death of his father constituted more than an emotional trauma for Wu Ching-tzu; it also placed on his youthful shoulders the complex burden of running a household and settling the estate, practical tasks to which he was by nature unsuited. Ch'eng Chin-fang (1718–1784), a distant relative and benefactor and one of his most important biographers, tells us that Wu's inheritance was worth over twenty thousand taels of gold, an amount sufficient to provide him with a false sense of material security and to attract various designing claimants.[21] What actually happened is described only in poetic metaphor, but we can gather from various accounts that greedy relatives ("evil-sounding kite-owls" and "wolves") stirred up much conflict, and that Wu would rather diminish his estate and satisfy their demands than stoop to contend with them.[22] Troubled by these unfamiliar cares, Wu began to seek escape in the pleasures of wine, sex, and song—things amply available in the gay quarters along the Ch'in-huai River which flows through Nanking, China's southern capital and easily reachable by water from Wu's home.

In terms of Wu Ching-tzu's growth as an artist, this interlude of dissipation in his life was not at all unfruitful. In Nanking, he fell into the company of actors, at the time considered no more respectable in society than the prostitutes with whom they commingled. But these actors were not without admirable skills, and Wu soon learned enough from them to become known for the dramatic lyrics he contributed to their repertoire. And years later, even as he poetically recalled this time of his life in a tone of regret ("Money by his pillow gone, the young man tenders greetings with shame on his face"), he remained proud of his reputation as a fine writer of popular lyrics ("West of Pai-pan Bridge, he earned a name for talent among the dramatists").[23] This expert acquaintance with the world of popular entertainment was later put to good use in the crafting of his novel, which also features realistic descriptions of actors and prostitutes. But more important, Wu's pleasure-seeking experiences gave him a respect for and a love of popular literature and were undoubtedly influential in his eventually choosing a form of it—fiction writing—for his greatest work.

In terms of Wu's immediate welfare, however, these revels soon proved detrimental. To continue his life of pleasure, Wu was eventually forced to sell most of his family's holdings as his reserves dwindled away. Whatever guilt or regret he might have felt he waited to express in his poetry; to those around him, he maintained an exterior of stubborn unconcern. In 1729 Wu Ch'ing wrote:

> Last year you sold your fields and now your house,
> And the old folks are mumbling their bitter complaints.
> But you with folded hands fend them off,
> Your eyebrows like halberds, your voice a tiger's roar.[24]

But the hard fact was that, only six years after his father's passing, Wu Ching-tzu had squandered away most of the family estate and found himself on the threshold of poverty. And along with the decline of his wealth came a decline in the respect he commanded in the community. The townspeople of Ch'üan-chiao began to ridicule him for his prodigal ways, and there is much evidence in Wu's poetry to show that this produced in him a reaction of both hurt and anger. In early 1731, while away from home on the eve of the lunar New Year (which, for that year, corresponds to February 6), he wrote a series of lyrics to the abbreviated form of the tune "Mu-lan hua" in which he reviewed this period in a mood of self-pity. Among them is the following:

> My land and houses all sold,
> In local circles, I serve as warning to son and brother.
> That young so-and-so,
> Astride his fat horse, in his fluffy furs, smiles on my poverty!
> I'll find a mountain and hide,
> But my soul is not steady like streams and valleys.
> Coming this time south of the Yangtze,
> My exile and my poverty are both unbearable.[25]

In the same series, he recalled his father's passing ("Nine years since he ascended to heaven") and vowed to follow in his path,

"Clutching in my hands his canons, weeping tears of blood."[26] His lament continued for his "mild, toilworn mother" who still lay unburied in a "desolate coffin," because he was not yet able to secure a suitable grave site where his parents could lie side by side. Moreover, as if to compound his troubles, his young wife had died around 1728, leaving him with at least one infant son.[27] Wu's self-pity and frustration are overwhelming in the verse recounting this misfortune:

> She's dead and gone from the bridal chamber,
> And I grieve over the past in the chill of the courtyard.
> I have but a kitchen maid now
> Whose clumsiness erases the sweet memory of my dead helpmate.
> When melancholy comes, I gaze in the mirror
> And see two haggard strands on the sides of my face.
> Would that I could find a good match,
> But who would be willing to wake this Chiang-lang
> from his slumber?[28]

"Chiang-lang" in the last line refers to Chiang Yen (444–505), a gifted litterateur and high official of the Liang dynasty (502–557) who, according to legend, first returned some silk and then a multicolored brush to different visitors in dreams and awoke to find that his literary talents had left him. In thus calling himself Chiang-lang, Wu was indicating the fading away of his early promise, a rather astounding conclusion for a man of just thirty.

We do not know exactly what brought about this self-deprecating judgment, but we do know that Wu was to progress no further in the civil service examinations than the lowly *sheng-yuan* (or, more colloquially, *hsiu-ts'ai*) degree he had earned in 1723. The likelihood is that, even during those years of reckless pleasure seeking, he continued, if only in a lackadaisical fashion, to aspire to success in the examinations. After all, such success would have been a way out of his problems of encroaching poverty and the malicious gossip that followed. In 1729, his cousin Chin Liang-ming tells us, he was still reporting to the government examiner at Ch'u-chou (which had jurisdiction over Ch'uan-chiao) to take one of the periodic examinations which determined the promotion, demotion, or dismissal of *sheng-yüan*.[29] Although Wu did pass, his eccentric behavior did not escape the examiner's notice and he suffered through the indignity of a reprimand. There is no mention anywhere of whether Wu ever proceeded to the important provincial (*chü-jen*) examination, the passing of which would have qualified him for a government post. We merely know that he left his hometown to reside in Nanking permanently in 1733 and seems to have ceased any further participation in the examination system at about the same time. Like his fictionalized hero Wang Mien in the *Ju-lin wai-shih*, he died without holding office "even for a single day."

Wu Ching-tzu's feelings about conventional success, especially in light of the ridicule he heaped upon it in his satire, have been a subject of constant debate among his latter day biographers. Did Wu, as many of his Marxist admirers insist, deliberately detach himself from the system he criticizes so severely in his novel, or did he, as Hu Shih suggests, become a bitter convert to his satirical role only when he saw that all paths to conventional success were closed? The evidence at hand is insufficient to settle the question, but we do know from Wu's interpretation of the significance of his father's life that he had a high regard for an idealistic commitment to Confucian virtues—his youthful abandonment to a period of dissolute living notwithstanding—a commitment which would enjoin him from compromising the cultivation of morality and intellect to the requirements of practical gain. As we shall see, this became the moral theme of the *Ju-lin wai-shih*. On the other hand, we should also realize that, to most men of his time, passing the examinations and holding office constituted the ultimate goal in life, and was both sanctioned by the Confucian canons and rewarded by wealth and fame. To forsake this goal, whatever the justification, could not have been a simple decision, and we should not be surprised to find in Wu Ching-tzu's poetry a recurring sense of guilt and self-condemnation for having done so. Wu might have revered his father for the latter's self-cultivation, but he also remained proud of his ancestors who led distinguished lives in service to the state. His decision to follow in what he saw as his father's path, whether deliberate or forced, could not have been free from innate tensions between the idealistic and the practical sides of the Confucianist philosophy which guided him throughout his life. Even in the satire he was later to write, vestiges of these tensions remain to baffle critics who insist on simple values and consistent attitudes. This point will become clear as we examine the moral meaning of the *Ju-lin wai-shih* in a later chapter.

IV   *The Move to Nanking*

No one knows exactly when Wu Ching-tzu decided to seek examination honors no longer. The year 1733 is a likely one, because his autobiographical poems written about this time begin to be laced with references to recluses and to a life of retirement. 1733 is also the year he moved from his native Ch'üan-chiao to Nanking, to a house by the Ch'in-huai River close to the scene of his earlier revelries. Biographers from Hu Shih onward have cited his disgust for the gossipy people of Ch'üan-chiao as the reason for the move, and they have pointed out that this hatred shows up years later in the *Ju-lin wai-shih's* fictional account of the materialistic, superstitious, and inhumane residents of Wu-ho *hsien*. But from the "Yi-chia *fu*" and other poems of this period, it appears that the move was also occasioned by his intention to give up the examination life and to live out his days in leisurely pursuits. In Nanking, a cultured and sophisticated metropolis, Wu would better be able to follow this route free from the censure and the insults which plagued him in provincial-minded Ch'üan-chiao. His move, therefore, was made in a mood of painful sadness not just because it represented self-exile: Nanking is after all not very far from Ch'üan-chiao and there is ample evidence that Wu loved the city. This sadness was profound and real because the move also represented to him the end of his worldly aspirations. In the "Yi-chia *fu*," written in "extreme grief and resentful anger, with copiously flowing tears," he alludes to scores of historical examples of loss of talent and ambition and restates his resolve to end his days quietly in his urban hideaway. The tone of resignation grows even stronger in two lyrics to the tune "Mai p'i-t'ang" written at the welcoming party given him by Nanking friends upon his arrival; the second one ends as follows:

In the world of men
It's only glory that withers easily,
While love and concern by nature die hard.
I bought on whim this house on a bank of the Ch'in-huai,
And now I truly feel it's superior to country living.
While starving to death,
One doesn't seem to mind occasionally washing coarse rice.
I will now withdraw myself,

Beckoning to friends like Juan Chi and Hsi K'ang,[30]
Who, opening their collars and hunkering down,
Will drink with me into a deep stupor.[31]

While one can indeed detect a lingering discontent (in lines 6 and 7,
for example), his purpose in moving to Nanking is clear: to take up
the life of a recluse, to forget his sorrows in the company of superior
friends. At thirty-two, an age when most men of talent are at the
peak of their careers, Wu Ching-tzu has thus bade farewell to the
active life. While the justification for this was later expressed in the
Ju-lin wai-shih, it is easy to see why Wu retained for some time
feelings of guilt and doubt about his premature retirement.[32]

Wu's life in Nanking, despite the grinding poverty that soon became his lot, was not altogether dreary. He had a new wife with him
and fathered more sons.[33] And Chin Ho, a later biographer, reports
that, whatever his finances, he entertained "men of wine and literature from everywhere who ventured into Nanking."[34] He also
traveled widely throughout the area, spending much time especially
in Yang-chou (Yangchow).[35] His circle of literary friends widened,
and he enjoyed a burgeoning reputation for scholarship and literary
talent. It was this reputation that brought on the next major event in
his life, an event which ultimately turned him from a somewhat
reluctant recluse to a full-blown satirist defending the life of withdrawal by criticizing the conditions surrounding those who remained active.

V   *The Recommendation of 1736*

Just three years after moving to Nanking, Wu Ching-tzu was
given an unexpected opportunity—the last in his life—to return to
the examination life he thought he had given up for good: he was
recommended for a special government examination known as the
Po-hsüeh hung-tz'u, or "Great Literary Scholarship."[36]

As the name suggests, this examination, ordered convened by the
new Ch'ien-lung emperor, sought to ferret out men of talent and
worth in the land, to be recommended by high government officials.
Candidates would go through a more simplified version of the regular examinations and be tested on their knowledge of the classics and
history as well as on their ability to compose poetry and essays.
Those who passed would be immediately eligible for high office,
thus bypassing the far more tedious regular route.[37]

By this time, Wu's reputation had grown sufficiently well to be known to the officials of his district. His name was recommended to both the governor and the chief education officer of Anhwei province, and, early in 1736, he took a preliminary test administered by the governor to determine the candidates to be recommended for the examination in Peking. Wu evidently did well, but just as the process of recommendation was about to be completed, he withdrew his name from consideration, citing illness as the reason.

There is an ongoing dispute in current scholarship over whether Wu Ching-tzu was actually ill or only pretended to be so; the available evidence is insufficient to determine definitely one way or the other. We do have a preface to the *Wen-mu shan-fang chi* written by T'ang Shih-lin, the education officer in Nanking who first submitted Wu's name to other high officials; in it T'ang recalls Wu's last minute withdrawal and includes the following: "Two months later, he recovered from his illness and visited my studio. . . . I observed that his countenance was haggard and drawn, and [it appears that] he had not feigned illness in declining [the recommendation]."[38] While Hu Shih and others have taken this account to be conclusive evidence that poor health did in fact prevent Wu Ching-tzu from following through with this last chance for worldly success, many who are intent on attributing altruistic principles to Wu's later criticism of the whole system insist that the excuse Wu offered was made up and that his decision not to compete was made freely and not forced on him by circumstances beyond his control. After all, they point out, T'ang Shih-lin's statement amounts to only a judgment on his part, made a long two months after the fact.

The point is not important enough to justify the amount of ink already expended in its discussion. Suffice it to say that, after this final opportunity, Wu remained in Nanking, determined now more than ever to live out his days in the manner of a Confucian recluse, to devote his time to the study of history, poetry, and the classics, to the enjoyment of wine and camaraderie, and to traveling about the cities and towns of the region, considered to be the loveliest of all of China. We have evidence, in the form of a poem written on the eve of the following lunar New Year (January 30, 1737), that even then he was not without regrets. This poem, like many Wu has written, is highly allusive and difficult to decipher, and its interpretation is also under dispute.[39] But in it Wu is clearly complaining about his inability to satisfy his basic material needs: he cannot afford even a

chicken for his holiday fare. He alludes to Ssu-ma Hsiang-ju (179–
117 B.C.), the great Han dynasty *fu* poet who, even in his final
illness, wrote his famous essay on imperial sacrifices; and he recalls
Tung Chung-shu (179?–104? B.C.), who answered *his* emperor's call
and authored a metaphysical system enshrining Confucianism as the
state philosophy. Why have I refused my emperor, Wu asks, and
brought myself to such straits?[40] Then he sighs at the frustrations of
his life:

> Nothing goes right in my life;
> Everything slips away.
> I'm like a bird caught in a net,
> Unable to stretch my feathers. [41]

But the profound bitterness, so evident in the "Yi-chia *fu*," is gone,
and the self-pity even gives way to a touch of self-mockery. Lingering regrets and all, Wu was finally settling down to his eremitic
existence, finally beginning to put aside his aspirations for position
and gain. With this resignation, his idealistic side came to the fore,
and he marked his final commitment to Confucianism by contributing his remaining capital to a sacrificial ceremony honoring a legendary sage and making this ceremony the moral centerpiece of the
pioneering work of satire he would complete to explain and justify
this commitment.

VI   *The Temple Sacrifices*

Many of Wu Ching-tzu's biographers mention that some years
after moving to Nanking he took part in a project to restore a dilapi-
dated shrine to the Confucian sage T'ai-po on Rain Flower Terrace
(Yü-hua T'ai), a piece of high ground which overlooks the south gate
of the city. Undoubtedly this was the project which inspired the
account of the T'ai-po sacrifices, described in such tedious detail in
Chapter 37 of the *Ju-lin wai-shih*. Scholars from Hu Shih on have
taken as authority for this incident the account of Wu's life in the
local gazetteer of Ch'üan-chiao (*Ch'üan-chiao hsien chih*) and Chin
Ho's postscript to the 1869 Su-chou (Soochow) edition of the *Ju-lin
wai-shih*, largely ignoring the slight discrepancy between the two. [42]
If we were to reread the various accounts of Wu Ching-tzu's life, we
might indeed wonder why such an important event was not mentioned at all by Ch'eng Chin-fang, the one source that would be

most reliable, inasmuch as Ch'eng is the only biographer who was also a close friend of Wu's. Moreover, even though it is undeniable that Wu patterned many of his characters in the *Ju-lin wai-shih* after real persons and derived many of his subplots from actual events of the day, his usual habit was to fictionalize, to change names and alter occurrences in some fashion.[43] We might therefore expect that the T'ai-po incident too would have been different from the way it was reported in the fictional narrative.

A source better than those previously available was uncovered in Hunan province in 1956, in the form of twenty-three poems on various famous places of Nanking which Wu Ching-tzu wrote in 1753, just a year before his death. Among them is one describing Rain Flower Terrace, and the following lines appear near the end of the preface: "In a recent year, a temple to Ts'ang Chieh was built below the ridge [of the Terrace]. The gentry and officials of the city used a bullock and sweet wine to offer sacrifices in the temple, playing ancient music, and putting on ritual dancing; the entire city went to see it." And the poem, an "ancient style" composition in five-syllable lines, ends with the following couplet: "The people of the capital participated in ceremonies and music here,/Taking the occasion to pay homage to Ts'ang Chieh."[44] Thus from the most reliable source of all, Wu Ching-tzu himself, we learn that the actual sacrifices on which the T'ai-po incident was based were not to T'ai-po at all, but really to Ts'ang Chieh, the legendary inventer of Chinese writing.[45] So it appears that when the Ch'üan-chiao gazetteer and Chin Ho reported that the ceremonies on Rain Flower Terrace were made to T'ai-po, they were merely following the fictionalized account in the *Ju-lin wai-shih*, the incidents in which, a century or so after Wu's death, were already being confused with actual events in Wu's life.

It can be argued that this distinction is not worth making: whether it was to Ts'ang Chieh or to T'ai-po, all that is important to note is that Wu Ching-tzu spent his dwindling funds on a symbolic act. But in terms of our understanding of the *Ju-lin wai-shih*, it is highly significant to note the direction of the author's fictionalization. Wu Ching-tzu changed the sage honored from Ts'ang Chieh to T'ai-po for a reason; ascertaining that reason would be one important step toward ascertaining the moral basis of Wu's satire, still a point of dispute among critics of the novel.

According to legend, T'ai-po was the eldest son of King Tan, the ancestor of the sovereigns of the Chou dynasty (1122–265 B.C.), the earlier part of which was considered by Confucius as the last of China's three golden ages and the time when the classical virtues he preached were actually practiced in human society. T'ai-po himself embodied the virtue of *jang*, or "yielding," because he was said to have fled to the then barbaric Wu region (an area which includes Nanking) in order to yield the throne to a younger brother; to his arrival was attributed the civilizing of all of southeastern China.[46] Wu Ching-tzu's account of the honoring of T'ai-po, far from merely recording an actual event, can now be seen as a deliberate device to explain the moral basis of his satirical work: for the virtue of *jang* is the one most opposed to the competitive quest for wealth and status which the system of civil service examinations and officeholding perpetuated. The relevance of this point will become clear in Chapter 3, when we examine the moral basis of the satire in the *Ju-lin wai-shih*.

VII   *The* Ju-lin wai-shih

No one has yet been able to determine exactly the time Wu Ching-tzu began, probably as a kind of leisurely activity, to set down the moral justification of his life in a work of satirical fiction. The usual estimate is between 1736 and 1740, often for the reason that Wu never gave up the idea of participating in the examination system he criticizes in his novel until after the *Po-hsüeh hung-tz'u* recommendation of 1736. But if, as we have seen, Wu's ambivalent attitude toward the conventional route to success originated in his early appreciation of the idealistic virtues of his father, then it is possible that parts of the work could have been written much earlier, perhaps even during his sojourn with his father in Chiang-su. Most likely, however, the bulk of the *Ju-lin wai-shih* took shape between the mid-1730s and the mid-1740s, after he had become quite settled in his Nanking existence. On this point, we have the word of Wang Yu-tseng (1736–1762), a classmate of Wu's eldest son and an admirer of Wu's poetry, that "From his days of leisure sitting in front of Chung Hill,/He conceived the details of the *Ju-lin wai-shih*."[47] Chung Hill is a well-known part of Nanking and, in these lines, becomes a synecdochical symbol of the city. And even though the geographical setting of the *Ju-lin wai-shih* is the various towns and cities of the lower Yangtze plain, Nanking remains the point of focus, the primary location where its fictional scholars gather. [48] This circumstantial fact meshes with Wang Yu-tseng's lines; from both we can at least make an educated estimate of when and where Wu Ching-tzu wrote his famous novel.

Like his contemporary Ts'ao Hsüeh-ch'in (1716?–1763), the author of the celebrated *Red Chamber Dream* (*Hung-lou meng*), Wu Ching-tzu also wrote for the amusement of his friends. Manuscript copies of the *Ju-lin wai-shih*, in complete or partially completed form were passed around in Nanking literary circles until, as Wu's friend Ch'eng Chin-fang attests in the poem quoted earlier, Wu became known principally as a writer of vernacular fiction. Ch'eng's poem can be ascertained to have been written between 1748 and 1750 and, since Hu Shih's pioneering study, the *Ju-lin wai-shih's* existence has been dated to those years. It remained in manuscript form until Chin Chao-yen (b. 1718), another friend and relative of the author, published it some time during his tenure as an education official in Yang-chou between 1768 and 1779. [49]

Despite its popularity, it is doubtful whether Wu Ching-tzu derived much immediate benefit from what turned out to be his most important work. Nor would he have expected to: fiction in the vernacular, even for aficionados, was little more than casual entertainment for oneself and one's friends. We can be certain that Wu Ching-tzu, in choosing this form of expression for his ideas, was also interested in providing his readers with a laugh or two: there is ample humor in the *Ju-lin wai-shih*. But he was too moralistic a person, too Confucianist in outlook, not to infuse this humor with didactic design. The result is the first sustained satire in Chinese narrative fiction, a work which secures for Wu Ching-tzu the lasting fame he thought he had given up forever when he withdrew from the competitive path to government service.

VIII *Wu Ching-tzu's Later Years*

Wu Ching-tzu, as has already been indicated, probably completed the *Ju-lin wai-shih* during the fifth decade of his life. But because the autobiographical poems in the extant *Wen-mu shan-fang chi* cover only his first forty years, we are left with only the accounts of others on his life thereafter. These accounts usually stress two things: the stark poverty which plagued Wu to the end of his days, and the indomitable spirit, so different from the self-pity and self-doubt of his earlier poetry, with which he confronted his misfortunes. To his biographers at least, he seems to have achieved in his later years a certain peace from his earlier doubts about the life of retirement and to have settled down to the life of the Confucian eremitic he defends in the *Ju-lin wai-shih*.

Ch'eng Chin-fang relates that, after giving up the examination life for good in 1736, Wu Ching-tzu became even poorer.[50] Ch'eng does not give the reason for this, but later biographers have tied Wu's final destitution to the sale of his house to finance the temple sacrifices.[51] We know also, from another friend's poem, that Wu maintained a house in East Water Gate (Tung-shui kuan) near Huai-ch'ing Bridge for over ten years after his arrival in Nanking.[52] If these sources are reliable, then we can conclude that Wu took part in the temple sacrifices after 1743, when he also sold his house. By Ch'eng Chin-fang's account, Wu then moved to a desolate place near Ta-chung Bridge east of the Yangtze where he occupied himself day and night with volumes of old books he had brought along. When without funds, he would exchange these books for rice. Occasionally he was able to earn something from his literary skills, by composing poetry and writing essays for those who would pay for them. Ch'eng relates the following incident as an illustration of the dire straits into which Wu had fallen in middle age: "My great-uncle Li-shan was related to him by marriage and periodically aided him. Early one autumn, after it had been raining hard for three or four days, my great-uncle told his sons, 'The rice in town today must be unusually expensive. I wonder how Min-hsüan is doing? You may take three bushels of rice and two thousand cash and go see how he is.' When they arrived, he had not eaten for two days."[53] By such handouts from relatives and friends and by an occasional job, Wu eked out a living while constantly hovering on the edge of starvation. But to the admiration of his friends, he maintained a cheerful exterior, "as if he did not realize that he was first rich and then became poor."[54] Whenever he managed to acquire some money, Ch'eng Chin-fang tells us, he would quickly spend it on wine and merrymaking and "never worry about tomorrow." Once, while he was visiting Ch'eng, the latter was surprised to find that he had neither writing brush nor inkstone with him. "These things are what our kind depends on for a livelihood," Ch'eng said to him. "How could you be without them for even a short while?" "My brush and ink are within my bosom," Wu replied. "So don't fuss about such things."

In the dead of winter, lacking food and wine for his belly and fuel for his stove, Wu would gather five or six good friends to counter the bitter cold of night by walking outside the city walls under the moonlight, singing and shouting to each other, and not reentering the city until the dawn when they would part company amid loud laughter. They called this activity *nuan-tsu*, or "warming the feet."

Incidents like these have tended to foster the impression that Wu Ching-tzu was strongly influenced by Taoism, a philosophy which holds to the ultimate relativity of all values and which expresses itself in an iconoclastic defiance of social conventions.[55] This interpretation of his philosophical outlook is linked to the interpretation of his novel, which will be discussed at length in the following chapters. For the present, however, it is important to see that Wu's behavior in later life, as eccentric as it may seem, was not characterized by an undisciplined abandon or by a thoroughly relativistic view of life. For, if anything, Wu spent even more time in the study of the Chinese classics during his Nanking days than he did in his youth, and he was explicit in his defense of the Confucian values they uphold. Ch'eng Chin-fang notes that in the later part of Wu's life, he became fond of annotating the classics and quotes him as saying that "in them are the foundations of human life." In one of Wu's two extant prose essays, written not long before his death as a preface to a "private study" of the *Book of History (Shang shu)* by his friend Chiang Yü (1706–1770), we find Wu Ching-tzu equating "the classics of the sages" to "the sun and moon in the heavens," illuminating the myriad changes of earthly existence.[56] Such statements would be alien indeed to anyone with a Taoist orientation. Wu Ching-tzu did withdraw from the active life that most Confucians pursue; but we can be sure that this withdrawal was not brought about by any loss of faith in Confucian principles. On the contrary, we find him upholding the uncompromising practice of these principles—of filial piety, self-cultivation, and moral and intellectual integrity—as the bases for his satire. In his life as in his fiction, the justification for withdrawal from service to society was the idealistic commitment to certain moral and intellectual values which must otherwise be compromised, not the nihilistic denial of those values.

Wu's relative Chin Chao-yen, who would later publish the *Ju-lin wai-shih*, has left us a long poem which provides a good portrait of Wu Ching-tzu in his twilight years:

> How lofty is Master Wen-mu,
> Still lost in books at age fifty.
> He looks for the remnants of the sages in boats and houses,
> And seeks out Confucious and Fu-hsi among bamboo cutters
>   and sellers of sauces. . . .[57]
> Those who, with great deference, seek the way to his humble hut,
> Find him hidden there, away from human recognition.
> There are times when, with his hat on upside down,
> He drinks alone at a Ch'in-huai tavern.
> And neighborhood children, when they chance upon him,
> All say he's inflicted with madness incurable.[58]

Wu indeed became a thorough eccentric, but definitely a Confucianist one, "lost in books" and searching everywhere for the wisdom of the ancients. His studies of the Confucian classics, especially of the *Book of Poetry (Shih ching)* for which he wrote a commentary, gave him a sense of worth, while his steadfast refusal to seek public office gave him an aura of transcendence over those who continued to compete.

IX *The Final Days*

Wu's material fortunes, however, never improved. His talented eldest son Wu Lang became an official in 1751 but, for unspecified reasons, was unable to relieve his father's financial needs.[59] In late autumn of 1754, Wu met Ch'eng Chin-fang in Yang-chou, at a time when Ch'eng too was suffering through destitute days after having once been wealthy. Wu grasped Ch'eng's hand in sympathy and said, "You too have come to be like me. It's not easy to cope with this kind of life; but what can one do?" Only days later, before he could return to Nanking, Wu Ching-tzu was dead.

The circumstances of his death have been recorded in both prose and verse, though there is some disagreement as to the exact date.[60] The most reliable account appears to be that of Wang Yu-tseng; Wang claims to have visited with Wu on the afternoon of the fateful day, which he gives as December 11, 1754 (the twenty-eighth day of the tenth moon in the year *chia-hsü*). That evening Wu returned to the boat in which he was traveling, consumed a flagon of wine, and died soon after going to bed, probably from a stroke. Just a few days earlier, he had "gathered together the remaining cash in his purse" to invite friends to drink with him. Flushed with liquor, he recited a quatrain from the ninth-century poet Chang Hu which included the line "A man is born to die fittingly only in Yang-chou." Ch'eng Chin-fang, who recorded the incident, marvels at how soon this came true for his friend. In his account, however, Ch'eng mistakenly attributes the line to Tu Mu (803–852), a more famous poet contemporary with Chang, and thus missed the further significance of Wu's recitation. For Chang Hu, during the Ch'ang-ch'ing period of the T'ang dynasty (821–823), also refused a recommendation to an official position and ended his days as a recluse.[61] Thus, to the very end of his life, Wu Ching-tzu never stopped relating himself to other high-minded men in Chinese history who opted for the eremitic life.[62] This fact will prove helpful as we try later on to unravel the moral message of the *Ju-lin wai-shih*.

After his death, Wu Ching-tzu's mortal remains were transported back to Nanking through the help of Lu Chien-tseng (1690–1768), then the rich and powerful chief salt commissioner of the area and another of Wu's acquaintances.[63] It is reported that Wu was interred among the flowers by Phoenix Terrace Gate (Feng-t'ai men), in the fields to the south of the city he loved.[64]

X   *The Immediate Family*

Facts which came to light after Hu Shih's chronological biography show that Wu Ching-tzu was married at least twice. His first wife, the mother of his eldest son, died around 1728, during the most unhappy years of his life.[65] Subsequently, he married a woman of the Yeh family of Ch'üan-chiao, whose father was a physician.[66] In his lifetime, Wu fathered a total of four sons. Wu Lang, the eldest (also known by his *tzu* of Hsün-shu and his *hao* of Shan-t'ing), was the most outstanding and evidently the favorite of his father.[67] Forced to provide for himself at a tender age because of his father's financial problems, Lang managed to attain the high official honors which had eluded his branch of the family for the three previous generations. In 1751, the Ch'ien-lung emperor made a tour of south China and proclaimed a special examination which Lang passed, thus obtaining his *chü-jen* degree. Soon thereafter, he was appointed a clerk in the grand secretariat in Peking, a position he held at the time of Wu Ching-tzu's death.[68] Lang is known to posterity as one of the leading mathematicians of his time, and it is from his extant poetry that modern scholarship has been able to determine various facts concerning his siblings.[69]

The given name of Wu Ching-tzu's second son is evidently lost; all that remains is his brother Lang's casual reference which gives his *tzu* as Li-shu and his *hao* as Chu-lang. This son died young, before Wu himself, and nothing else is known of him. Wu Ching-tzu's third son was Wu Wen-hsiung (*tzu*, Heng-shu; *hao*, Wei-ch'uan), who became a *chü-jen* in 1753, shortly before his father's death. Later he was promoted to the magistracy of P'u-ning in Ch'ao-chou. A fourth son is mentioned by Chin Chao-yen as being present at his father's death, "weeping at the head of the bed." His name is not to be found in Wu Lang's writings, but, from a writer's brief note of a meeting with him in 1768, it has been determined that he was Wu Ao who later studied at the Imperial College in Peking as a student on government stipend. Ao served in a number of official posts and, in 1777, was promoted to the magistracy of Tsun-hua chou, where he died the following year.[70]

Compared to their luckless father, therefore, Wu Ching-tzu's three surviving sons all attained a measure of conventional success, though none was able to advance to the first-rank officialdom of their illustrious ancestors. None, moreover, left as much of a name to posterity as their eccentric father whose original genius remains preserved in a work of satirical fiction that was destined for acclaim.

XI *Works Extant and Lost*

In a historical development Wu Ching-tzu could not have fore-seen, the movement to create a new literature in China gathered force in the 1920s as part of the larger movement to modernize and to deal with the new realities forced on the Chinese by nineteenth-century Western encroachment. As part of this movement, classical Chinese (*wen-yen*), the learned language of the literati, gave way to the vernacular (*pai-hua*), the everyday language of the common people, as the medium of literary expression.[71] Scholars like Hu Shih scoured the Chinese tradition for outstanding examples of ver-nacular literature which could serve as guides to aspiring young writers. Thus it happened that traditional fiction in the vernacular, long lightly regarded, was finally accorded a place of respect in Chinese literary history, and Wu Ching-tzu ultimately came to be known as the author of the *Ju-lin wai-shih*.

From our present perspective, we cannot say that this is unjust: Wu's extant works other than his satirical novel—the four *chüan Wen-mu shan-fang chi*, the recently discovered twenty-three poems praising the scenic spots of Nanking, two prose prefaces to the works of friends, four other poems discovered in recent years, plus a specimen of his calligraphy and imprints from his seals—hardly merit our aesthetic interest; they are valuable only insofar as they provide added information on his life, which, in turn, helps us to decipher the meaning of his satire.[72] Wu Ching-tzu's literary genius lies not in what remains of his classical poetry and prose, which are rather undistinguished, but in the work of vernacular fiction for which he is remembered.

The outline of Wu's life given above is by no means final or complete, and the possibility remains that other lost works may be recovered which will fill in its lacunae or overturn its conclusions. From what we presently know, the most important of these lost works would be the later, expanded version of the *Wen-mu shan-fang chi*, which incorporated the earlier four *chüan* version we have into a much larger work of twelve *chüan*, seven of which contain poetry and five prose. This later collection, unlike the extant one, contained Wu Ching-tzu's works written after 1740 and would have been invaluable for a determination of the thought and literary achievements of his later years. Unfortunately, it was never published, even though Wu Lang devoted some time to editing its contents after his father's death. Chin Ho claims that his family once had the manuscript; but it was lost during the great Chinese civil war known as the T'ai-p'ing Rebellion of 1850–1865.[73] All that remains today is a preface for this work, written by Shen Ta-ch'eng (1700–1771), and a long poem with preface, written as a sort of appendix by Wang Yu-tseng.[74]

Besides poetry, prose, and fiction, Wu Ching-tzu also expended much personal effort on the study of the Chinese classics. From this effort emerged the *Shih-shuo*, a seven *chüan* commentary on various poems in the *Book of Poetry*; but this work too was never published and has not been seen since the T'ai-p'ing Rebellion.[75] Most scholars agree that the brief commentary on the *Book of Poetry* in Chapters 34 and 49 of the *Ju-lin wai-shih* was probably based on conclusions expressed in the *Shih-shuo*, and we can conclude from this that while Wu's views here have their own originality, they do not leave the boundaries of orthodox Confucianism. Wu apparently also ventured into historiography, another time-honored subject for a Confucian scholar. We have a reference to a historiographical work entitled *Shih-Han chi-yi* ("A Record of Doubtful Points Concerning the *Records of the Grand Historian* and the *Histories of the Han Dynasty*"), which Wu began but never completed.[76] Impressions of Wu Ching-tzu's interpretations of historical facts can also be gleaned from the *Ju-lin wai-shih;* but since the *Shih-Han chi-yi* too is lost, we have little basis for speculating on Wu's thoughts concerning history itself.[77]

XII *Conclusion*

Works of literature may pass through a process of natural selection in which, with the passing of time, only the best survive. At least this seems to be the case with Wu Ching-tzu: most of his poetry, all of his literary criticism, and nearly all of his work on the classics have faded away; what remains is a work of satire which traditionally would have been listed last among all the others but which, in the end, earns him a place in Chinese letters he could not have known he would hold. We regard Wu Ching-tzu today not as a poet or a classicist, but as a satirist of uncommon skill and import.

From facts which this chapter has laid out, it is clear that his natural talent for satire would probably not have come to fruition but for certain circumstances—his father's lack of worldly success, his own youthful dissipations, his poverty—which combined with his moralistic character to turn him from a disillusioned young man to a mature critic of his society. He presented his criticism with a quiet and subtle wit, so that modern critics, unfamiliar with the concerns which motivated his creativity, are still unable to come to a satisfactory explanation of its meaning. According to these critics, Wu was a Confucianist, but with a Taoist tinge to his thinking; or he saw through the evils of "feudalistic" systems, but was limited by history. Much of Wu Ching-tzu's thought is indeed paradoxical; but it is paradoxical within the confines of Confucianism. If we bear this in mind as we consider the *Ju-lin wai-shih*, the moral meaning of his sometimes baffling novel will fall into place; and it is by grasping this moral meaning that we also begin to grasp Wu's witty indirection and ultimately the totality of his art.

To talk of a given morality as having an innate role in artistic creativity, as the Chinese have done and continue to do, is anathema to many modern critics who regard each work as a separate and unique exploration and who, as Mark Schorer observes, focus on technique as the sole means of discovering the consequences of that exploration.[78] In the analysis of satirical art, however, this approach can prove limiting. For satire sets out not so much to explore as to persuade; it is motivated less by the desire to seek out truth than the determination to transmit it. Because of this, circumstances dealing with a piece of satire, such as certain facts of the author's biography, have a more direct—and, I believe, valid—connection with the judgment of its artistic worth. This I hope to make evident in the following chapter, which precedes the examination of Wu Ching-tzu's satire with an excursion into the nature of satire itself.

CHAPTER 2

Satire and Feng-tz'u

SATIRE is one of those terms in literary criticism which is often bandied about but seldom defined with any clarity or precision. But because the major task of the remainder of this study is to examine the meaning and art of Wu Ching-tzu's satirical novel, it behooves us to begin by considering what satire really is, both in our own tradition and in the Chinese tradition under which our author lived and worked.

Whether they say so specifically or not, the more astute of those who talk about satire are generally aware of its two basic components: what the English satirist and critic John Dryden (1631–1700) calls its "moral doctrine" and its "well-mannered wit." Dryden gives this description in his landmark essay, "A Discourse Concerning the Original and Progress of Satire," written in 1692 and published the following year.[1] Recently, Alvin Kernan has explained that this essay "summarizes the attempts of Renaissance scholars to provide satire with a history and a definition" and, with all its weaknesses of organization and expression, is significant as an index of Western understanding of satire before this century.[2] The "well-mannered wit" and the "moral doctrine" are what Kernan calls "the two poles of satire," and proof that these poles continue to characterize the modern critic's concept of satire is found in the description offered by Northrup Frye. "Satire," Frye writes, "demands at least a token fantasy, a content which the reader recognizes as grotesque, and at least an implicit moral standard, the latter being essential to a militant attitude to experience." The "fantasy" corresponds to Dryden's "wit" and, like Dryden, Frye links it with a necessary morality in satire.[3]

In less explicit terms, the modern Chinese litterateur Lu Hsün (Chou Shu-jen, 1881–1936), writing as a literary historian, reveals a similar understanding in advancing his judgment that the *Ju-lin wai-shih* contains the first satire in Chinese fiction: "Wu Ching-tzu's *The Scholars* is the first novel in which a writer criticizes social abuses without any personal malice, directing his attack mainly on the literati. The style is warm and humorous, gentle and ironical. This must rank as China's first novel of social satire."[4] Lu Hsün explains that previous examples of satirelike attacks can be found in Chinese fiction dating as far back as the Tsin dynasty (265–420); but until the *Ju-lin wai-shih*, these attacks were nearly all particular and personal. To Lu Hsün, the *Ju-lin wai-shih* is genuine satire because it departs from personal animosity to evince a larger, more social, concern, a concern which corresponds to the morality of Dryden and Frye. This concern, moreover, is expressed in a style—warm, humorous, gentle, ironical—proper to it, or we may say "wit." Hence, Lu Hsün too understands satire to consist of morality expressed in wit.

This is a sufficient definition for the discussion of most works of satire. But in the case of the *Ju-lin wai-shih*, we are dealing with a pioneering effort in which the author sometimes betrays his uncertainty by relaxing his focus and control. To delineate the work's one outstanding feature, its basic satirical import, we must sharpen our definition further by specifying satire's boundaries, by making as clear as possible what satire is not.

I   *Pure Humor and Satire*

In his truly insightful discussion, Northrup Frye explains that "the humor of pure fantasy" constitutes one boundary of satire. By "pure fantasy," Frye apparently means something immediately beyond the realm of actual experience, since he cites the incident of Alice encountering the White Knight in *Through the Looking-Glass* as an example.[5] Yet, even here, Frye writes that we can "sniff the acrid, pungent smell of satire" if we take the account as an allegory which can pull fantasy back into implicit connection with experience: the White Knight, who feels that one "should be provided for everything" and thus puts anklets around his horse's feet to guard against sharks (seeming fantasy), goes on to sing an elaborate parody of Wordsworth (unmistakable satire). The humor of satire is thus seen to be connected to actual experience, because satire must have an object of attack intelligible to an outside audience. The "humor of pure fantasy" is not satire because it does not attack, for it is involved not with any incongruity of real experience but with its own self-contained brand of fun. Frye apparently adds "pure fantasy" as a qualification because he sees that humor is founded on convention, and humor's tendency to take note of convention can at least be implicitly taken to be a form of attack. Still, in distinguishing humor from satire, the qualification is not necessary if the critic is willing (as Frye may not be) to make a judgment as to the aim or intention of a particular piece of writing. Humor in its pure state is that which sets out to make fun for its own sake, with no interest in denigration or ridicule. Satire, on the other hand, uses humor only as a means of attack, to stress its moral point via denigration and ridicule. The humorist may see the world as incongruous, but rather likes it that way. The satirist considers these same incongruities intolerable and sets out to correct them by persuading his audience of their undesirability. Humor then is to satire as a means is to an end. Satire uses humor as a tool so often that the two can easily be lumped together. Yet it is entirely possible, as in George Orwell's grim *1984*, to have pungent satire without much humor, just as humor, as in many of Alice's adventures, can occur without much satire.[6]

I hasten to add that this distinction between humor (or amoral wit) and true satire is much easier to state in theory than to apply in practice: we can never be absolutely sure of the intention of a work and, as critics, we are called upon in every case to make judgments which, while they should always be reasonable, do not carry the satisfaction of unshakable certitude. Moreover, it is important to recognize that these judgments are impossible to render without going outside of the text itself: Frye would never have known about the satirical features of the White Knight's song had he not also known about Wordsworth. This crucial point will be taken up again later.

From the distinction we have now made, we can determine various places in Wu Ching-tzu's novel where the desire to make fun overtakes the need to criticize, and where the story moves temporarily outside the realm of satire into the arena of pure humor. One of the most obvious of such examples occurs in Chapter 10, in which the reader is treated to a series of accidents at a wedding feast described in pure slapstick comedy:

When they had finished several cups of wine and two courses, the kitchen boy brought out the soup [on a tray]. Now this hired help was a country bumpkin. Wearing a pair of hobnail shoes and carrying six bowls of soupy noodles, he stood in the courtyard, bugging out his eyes as he watched the entertainment. The head steward had just served up four of the bowls, leaving the boy with two as he watched. At the sight of an actor on the stage twisting his torso in imitation of a singsong girl, the boy became carried away and forgot everything else. Thinking that all the bowls have been removed, he flipped the tray down so as to pour off any spilled soup. Ding-dong! The two bowls and their contents lay broken and scattered on the ground. Startled, he bent over to grab at the spillage, but found that the two dogs, smacking their lips and wagging their tongues, were trying to grab off the noodles and soup on the ground. Becoming furious, he stuck out a leg and kicked at them with all his might. Unexpectedly, he missed them, but having kicked too hard, he sent one of his hobnail shoes flying ten feet in the air.

Now Ch'en Ho-fu happened to be sitting at the first table on the left. On the table two plates of pastries—one of pork dumplings and the other of dumplings stuffed with goose fat and sugar—sat steaming hot. There was also a large, deep bowl of noodles and soup. He was just raising his chopsticks to his mouth when a black object hurtled round and round from behind the table and—p'ing-p'ing!—smashed the two plates of pastries to bits. Startled, Ch'en Ho-fu jumped up in fright, catching his sleeve on the bowl of soup and overturning it all over the table. . . .[7]

Even though the *Ju-lin wai-shih* can in general be called a sustained piece of satire, the passage above displays little more than pure humor and carries no value other than the fun it illustrates. This becomes clear if we take note of the obviously playful tone. The kitchen boy does not merely stare at the entertainment, but bugs out his eyes *(chien-che yen-ching)* as he watches. The actor on stage is not simply said to be acting out a woman's role, but as doing so while seductively *(niu-niu nieh-nieh ti)* twisting his torso. The dogs do not merely pounce on the spilled food, but also smack their lips and wag their tongues *(tsa-tsui nung-she ti)*. The pastries, awaiting the untimely arrival of the hobnail shoe, are not simply hot, but steamy with rising heat *(je-hung-hung ti)*; and the shoe, rather than just hurtling through the air, spins round and round *(ti-liu-liu ti)* before descending to ruin a tempting layout of food. The account, moreover, is complemented with onomatopoeia—"ding-dong!" and "p'ing-p'ing!"—to enhance the overall comic effect. Wu Ching-tzu may or may not have taken the idea for this episode from a T'ang dynasty historian, as Ho Tse-han suggests, but it is overwhelmingly clear that it is calculated to bring forth chuckles rather than sneers and thus falls short of genuine satire.[8]

In terms of Kernan's concept of the poles of satire, pure humor, which at least involves an intellectual perception of the incongruous, may be said to gravitate exclusively to the pole of wit; and it is for this reason that it can become confused with satire itself. Satire requires the interaction of this wit with moral indignation, and invective, which belongs entirely with the latter, can also be confused with satire.

II *Pure Invective and Satire*

In marking "pure denunciation" as satire's other boundary, Frye carefully notes that this boundary too is "very hazy" insofar as invective can be seen to carry wit and humor of its own. Nevertheless, the idea of pure, witless invective in theory is immensely useful as a means of helping us grasp the bipolar nature of satire itself. In the theoretical sense at least, pure invective is not satire, since it dwells exclusively on the morality pole and attacks without witty indirection. Its emotion is anger, pure and simple, without the rational detachment necessary for the exercise of satirical wit. As Frye points out, invective—such as calling a man a swine or a woman a bitch—covers a very limited range and affords "a severely restricted satisfaction." Still, Frye notes that "we like hearing people cursed" and "almost any denunciation, if vigorous enough, is followed by a reader with a kind of pleasure that soon breaks into a smile." Invectives heaped one upon the other, if artfully done, may indeed be one kind of wit and thus enter into the realm of satire. The telling difference is one of means: the curser is so intent on destroying his target that he employs invective, the most direct means available. The satirist may seek a similar end, but takes time to assume a more objective pose in pointing out the rational absurdities of the situation in order to cut deeper. In the context of an actual piece of writing, therefore, we are again called upon to make a judgment as to whether seeming invective is that and nothing more, or really a witty, indirect form of attack which would be properly labeled satire.[9]

Most of the episodes in the *Ju-lin wai-shih* can be said to be truly satirical inasmuch as they are free from direct artless attack. Nevertheless, we can cite at least one section in which anger so dominates the overall tone that the narrative slips frequently into invective. This is the section dealing with the town of Wu-ho (Chapter 44–48), a place many critics see as standing for Wu Ching-tzu's native Ch'üan-chiao. From the start, the sudden shift from satire to invective is obvious: "At this time, the P'eng family was on the upgrade in Wu-ho, having produced several metropolitan graduates, two of whom had been made members of the Han-lin Academy. "Since the people of Wu-ho were a narrow-minded lot, the whole county started playing up to these P'engs."

The other prominent family is the Fangs, salt merchants and pawnbrokers, who came from another town to "establish false residency" and who began to intermarry with the locals. The two old gentry families in town were at first unwilling.

But then there were some shameless and doltish men from these two families who, greedy for the Fangs' rich dowries, began to marry their daughters. . . . Thus among these two families, there were two types of men who cared nothing for the good name of their ancestors. The first type was fools who acted according to an eight-word dictum: "Not-Fang-not-marry; not-P'eng-not-friend." The other type was rascals who also conducted themselves according to eight words: "Not-Fang-not-think; not-P'eng-not-speak." That is to say, that had no Fangs claimed residency in Wu-ho, those shameless dolts would have done without wives; and had there been no P'engs who attained the *chin-shih* degree, they would have done without friends. This kind of people thought of themselves as wealthy and powerful, but actually they were stupid through and through.[10]

Name-calling, the most telltale of invectives, here rears its ugly head, and the contrast with real satire cannot be more stark. Clearly, our erstwhile satirist has allowed his anger to overtake his patience and thus largely forsakes the indirection of satirical wit for the direct assault of invective.

It should now be evident that just as humor corresponds to the "wit" pole of satire to form one boundary, invective corresponds to the "morality" pole to form the other. Satire, while clearly distinguishable from either extreme, can thus be seen as the dynamic interaction of both, leaning in particular cases to one pole or the other according to the satirist's penchant for anger or mirth. This interpretation can be diagrammed as follows:

Wit		SATIRE		Morality
(pure humor)	⟵⟶		⟵⟶	(pure invective)

In this scheme, the pole of wit, which stresses technique, is readily comprehensible to a modern critic; morality, on the other hand, cannot help but be involved with personal and social perceptions of reality or truth, and the understanding of its function in satire requires further distinctions.

III *Satire and Lampoon*

R. C. Elliott's monumental study of the origins of satire has established the link between primitive magical and ritual curses and the literary satire we encounter in later history.[11] In Elliott's view, satire began with something close to pure invective—the flytings of the Eskimos, the military curses of the Arabs, the "magical blasting spells" of the Irish—before the gradual distancing of the attacker from his work broadened the narrow moral focus of hard, personal attack and allowed the entrance of indirect wit which culminated in literary art.[12] This distancing, however, is infinitely variable: when it is sufficiently broad so that the moral focus encompasses a general, social situation, we have genuine satire; when it is sufficiently narrow and dwells on private grievances, we merely have lampoon.

The theoretical line between lampoon and invective is fuzzy enough to be ignored by certain critics, but the former may perhaps be distinguished from the latter by its regular use of sarcasm or humor as a means.[13] Invective, in the strictest sense, attacks directly and leaves no distance between the attacker and his attack; lampoon, while personal, does leave room for the ironic or humorous maneuverings of wit. Thus, while pure invective is clearly outside the realm of satire, lampoon can indeed be seen as satire's narrow-minded first cousin, different from satire only by its restricted moral vision.

In his essay on satire, Dryden clearly distinguishes between satires which espouse a general moral concern and satires "which were written against persons." The latter Dryden calls the "underwood of satire rather than the timber trees" because they "are not of general extension."[14] This personal kind of satire, "which is known in England by the name of lampoon," is not only not as "noble" as regular satire, but can be regarded as "a dangerous sort of weapon."[15] For, as Dryden explains in his inimitable way, "Some witty men may perhaps succeed to their designs, and, mixing sense with malice, blast the reputation of the most innocent amongst men, and the most virtuous amongst women."[16] Lampoon, then, can be seen as satire gone slightly awry; when satire becomes lampoon, what is usually written to reprehend "human vices, ignorance, and errors, and all things besides, which are produced from them" becomes instead a menace to the reputations of "the most innocent" or "the most virtuous" of individuals.[17]

This distinction between satire and lampoon establishes an important point regarding the morality of satire: that this morality must be broad and must direct itself toward general vice and folly rather than toward individuals. Attacks against individuals may indeed show a great deal of indirection and wit; but unless they are aimed at faults or foibles of some general extension, many critics would not consider them genuine satire. Jonathan Swift was surely thinking of this distinction when he wrote of himself as a satirist: "Yet, Malice never was his Aim;/He lash'd the Vice but spar'd the Name."[18]

The problem, however, does not end here. To say that the moral nature of satire calls for the general condemnation of vice and folly rather than for the expression of personal malice still leaves unanswered the question of the scope of this condemnation. Many critics have noted satire's preference for the topical, for actual persons, places, and times. As Gilbert Highet puts it, satire tends to be "always concrete, usually topical, often personal. It deals with actual cases, mentions real people by name, or describes them unmistakably (and often unflatteringly), talks of this moment and this city, and this special, very recent, very fresh deposit of corruption whose stench is still in the satirist's curling nostrils."[19] If this is true, then the morality of satire can hardly go beyond the political and the immediate and satire's barbs can be seen to be directed only against temporary systems or situations and not against such unchanging constants as human nature. In this way, Swift's *Modest Proposal* is meaningful only in the context of Britain's eighteenth-century Irish policy, and Wu Ching-tzu's *Ju-lin wai-shih* cannot be separated from a consideration of China's systems of social advancement during the Ch'ing dynasty. There is an undeniable validity to this view, although it overly de-emphasizes satire's concomitant ability to comment on and criticize the human condition as a whole.[20] Satire may launch its moralistic attacks largely on topical issues, but the vice and folly it brings out can, in many cases, be regarded as a shared feature of all men, apart from culture, time and place.

Our task in this study, however, is to ferret out the meaning and art of one particular satirical work; to do so accurately, our focus must initially be on topical issues that make up the work's immediate concern. Before we can see the *Ju-lin wai-shih*'s moral

relevance to the world, we must first see its relevance to the actual
conditions it set out to attack, as well as the particular readership it
sought to persuade. Once we have grasped these immediate issues,
the general relevance, if any, will quickly become obvious.

IV *Truth and Rhetoric*

Since satire is moralistic literature, the discussion of its nature
cannot be complete without the consideration of its relationship to
truth. Highet discusses the problem under the general heading of
"The Distorting Mirror," thus expressing a common opinion among
many critics who consider distortion a fundamental characteristic of
satirical art.[21] It has been written, for example, that a satirist "needs
to be unfair, or angry, or immature, in order to be effective, for
satire is, in its concept and technique and very nature, an unfair and
distorted treatment of material."[22] These same critics note, on the
other hand, that satirists themselves insist that their art tells the
truth. Rabelais, for example, is quoted in the beginning of *Pantagruel* as willing to offer himself "body and soul, tripe and bowels, to a
myriad of devils" if the whole of his history contains even a single
word of falsehood.[23] This attitude is summed up nicely in lines by
the modern satirist Roy Campbell: "I too can hiss the hair on men
erect/Because my lips are venomous with truth."[24] To satirists,
therefore, satire is not a "distorting mirror" but a "steele glass"
reflecting with uncompromising honesty "images of a crazy
world."[25]

The contradiction is not all that difficult to resolve. While modern
critics especially have focused their attention on satirical wit or
technique, satirists, themselves are evidently more concerned with
the moral point they are trying to make. Satirical distortions—
exaggerations, caricatures—are no more than rhetorical techniques
which the satirist employs to impress upon his readers the truth of
his underlying message. What satire seeks to distort is never the
moral truth; on the contrary, it is willing to play with appearance
and to exaggerate in order to convey the moral effectively. To the
modern Chinese satirist Lao She (Shu Ch'ing- ch'un, 1898–1965),
for example, satire cannot afford to waste time with balanced or
realistic portrayals. "As long as we must satirize," he writes, "we
should do it with sting . . . "; for "Satire that is painless and bland is
tentamount to that which shirks satire's responsibility and which
cannot achieve educative results."[26]

Lao She is overstating his case, however. The pragmatic need of satire to "achieve educative results" need not always cause it to exaggerate or overportray; in particular cases, the satirist may choose a more subtle or realistic approach as more effective. For the most part, this is precisely the approach Wu Ching-tzu takes in his satire, and its effects will be discussed fully in a later chapter.

The point is that no matter whether the satirist exaggerates, portrays objectively, or even understates, his overriding objective is the effectiveness of his persuasion. Satire has been rightly called "the most consistently and effectively rhetorical" of all major types of literature.[27] It is this rhetorical character, in fact, that distinguishes satirical narrative from the more agnostic kind we encounter in realistic fiction. Satire does not set out so much to explore truth as to transmit it, and a satirist is more a preacher or a manipulator than a seeker. While his methods vary and may indeed include, as in Wu Ching-tzu's case, a good deal of realism, the critic should not lose sight of satire's basically didactic nature which, in seeking primarily to shape the attitude of the reader, inevitably displays a different artistry from that found in realism-oriented narrative. Because satire is rhetorical literature, its moral truth cannot be as private. To acquire the reader's assent and sympathy, the satirist must so present his material as to link up with the reader's experience or prejudice. The skill with which he does this, in fact, is what determines the success or failure of his art.

Pragmatic or didactic literature has sometimes been dismissed as antithetical to art by important and influential critics. Especially when this literature deals with topical or political issues, it can be labeled pejoratively as propaganda. Consider, for example, the words of René Wellek and Austin Warren:

From views that art is discovery or insight into the truth we should distinguish the view that art—specifically literature—is propaganda, the view, that is, that the writer is not the discoverer but the persuasive purveyor of the truth. The term "propaganda" . . . in popular speech . . . is applied only to doctrines viewed as pernicious and spread by men whom we distrust. The word implies calculation, intention, and is usually applied to specific, rather restricted doctrines or programs. So . . . one might say that some art (the lowest kind) is propaganda, but that no great art, or good art, or Art, can possibly be.[28]

As we have been defining it, satire is undoubtedly propaganda.

Whether satire—for example, the *Ju-lin wai-shih*—can be considered "great art, or good art, or Art" remains a question that the following study will attempt to answer.

We might begin the process by noting that moralistic or pragmatic concerns have been more constant companions than strange outsiders to the theory and practice of literature in traditional China.[29] While Wu Ching-tzu may be said to be a pioneer in his choice of a popular mode to express his moral concerns, the idea that it is proper and fitting to use literature as a didactic tool is old and orthodox. If Wu is radical in satirizing the ready compromise of the Confucian ideals using the lightly regarded *hsiao-shuo* mode, the concept itself of witty and indirect censure of moral wrongs—what the Chinese call *feng-tz'u*—can be traced to the dawn of Chinese literature and literary criticism.

V   Feng-tz'u *in Chinese Tradition*

In what is generally considered to be the first Chinese treatise dealing with the theory and criticism of literature, the "Tien-lun lun-wen" ("Discourse on Literature in *The Classical Discourses*") of Ts'ao P'i (187–226), we are told that "literary composition is involved in the great task of governing the nation" and is thus "an enduringly honorable thing."[30] This fundamental concept is reiterated in a second milestone of Chinese literary criticism, the oft-quoted *Wen-fu* (*Exposition on Literature*) of Lu Chi (261–303):

> The use of literature
> Lies in its conveyance of every truth . . . .
> It maps all roads and paths for posterity,
> And mirrors the images of worthy ancients,
> That the tottering Edifices of the sage kings of antiquity
>   may be reared again,
> And their admonishing voices, windborne since of yore,
>   may resume full expression. . . .
> Virtue it makes endure and radiate on brass and stone,
> And resound in an eternal stream of melodies ever renewed
>   on pipes and strings.[31]

This moral concern of literature is both topical and general in scope. In the topical sense, it refers to the political task of governing the nation. But, at least in the Confucian scheme of things, this immediate task is intimately connected with a more general concept of moral truth once practiced by "worthy ancients" and "sage kings of antiquity" and ever renewed in the everyday practices (including, of course, the practice of literature) of virtuous men and rulers. Often called the Tao, this moral truth is the first topic of discussion in the *Wen-hsin tiao-lung (The Literary Mind: Elaborations)* of Liu Hsieh (ca. 465–523), the most comprehensive work on literature in traditional China. In Liu's broad, cosmic view, there is really no conflict between the broader and the narrower conceptions of morality in literature. For man, because he is endowed with a conscious mind, is seen to form a trinity with heaven and earth. Just as the natural universe manifests itself in an array of beautiful patterns (*wen*), the conscious human mind also manifests itself in *wen*, the Chinese designation for literature. In this way, the cosmic, the natural, the moral, and the aesthetic in literature become united and indivisible. Both the ancients who established the classics and Confucius who transmitted them "embellished their literary compositions according to the mind of the Tao, and both established their doctrines by referring to divine principles." It is by thoroughly studying the "patterns of heaven" and the "patterns of men" that "they were able to make sense of the universe, to successfully establish principles governing human society, to glorify practical endeavors, and to make elegant words and meanings. Thus we know that the Tao leaves patterns [*wen*] via the sages, and the sages via literature [*wen*] make Tao manifest."[32]

Any piece of writing worthy to be called literature, therefore, is inextricably linked to the teachings of the sages, the *ching* or classics, by concensus the places where the Tao is preserved and made known to mankind.[33] But this Tao, as Liu Hsieh sees it, is not some otherworldly ideal legislated upon men from some superhuman deity like the Judeo-Christian God; rather, it is man's own workings in consonance with his nature as a fully equal member of the cosmic union with heaven and earth. Literature, like government, is the human pattern, just as constellations are the pattern of heaven and mountains and rivers the pattern of earth; all three patterns together reveal the Tao. The implications of these concepts for literature are many; for this study, we are concerned only with their relationship to the traditional Chinese understanding of satire.

The Tao of literature, thus connected to the natural workings of man, is seen to reveal itself in the everyday occurrences of the human world, particularly during the Golden Age of high antiquity

when the sages lived. While later men may slip from ancient ideals
of perfect government and all-truthful literature, these ideal
nevertheless continue to be human and therefore practical, attain-
able, and unceasingly intertwined with human affairs. When individual human actions fall short of the Tao, it is the moral task of the
virtuous to point out by their writings and remonstrations such
moral lapses to the offenders, so that, indeed, "the tottering
Edifices of the sage kings of antiquity may be reared again/And their
admonishing voices . . . may resume full expression." When this
task, so consonant with the traditional moralistic conception of
literature, is done by subjects to rulers, it is called *feng*, or criticism
through indirection.[34]

Recently, Donald Gibbs has traced the etymology of this important word which, when first written down as a literary concept,
appeared without its dintinguishing "speech" signific and was thus
identical to the word for "wind."[35] In early Chinese writings, this
word was semantically extended to signify "prevailing mood" or
"influence." Later, in the important late Han dynasty *Major Preface
to the Book of Poetry, feng's* sense of "influence" took on an actively
didactic connotation in which a distinction was drawn between that
of ruler to subject and subject to ruler: "Those in high position, by
means of *suasive force* [*feng*] transform those below them, and those
below, by means of *critical persuasion* [*feng*] seek to redirect [that
is, *tz'u*, 'prod,' 'needle'] those above them. . . . Thus (as for the
first principle of poetry) it is called Persuasion [*feng*]."[36] When used
in reference to the influence of subjects on their rulers, therefore,
feng becomes "critical persuasion" to "prod" or "needle" (*tz'u*) the
latter in conformity with the moral Tao. Because this prodding or
needling is thus directed to the powerful whose pride can easily be
hurt to the point of taking reprisals against their subjects, *tz'u* must
necessarily be carried out with indirection and finesse. The *Major
Preface* takes pains to explain that "In these endeavors [that is, the
tz'u, or prodding from subordinates], the principle feature is to be
artistry [*wen*] to render the criticism oblique. In this way, the one
who speaks out does so without offense, and yet the one criticized
hears enough to be warned." It is thus that the concept of *feng*,
which has behind it the moral force of the Confucian Tao, came to
be associated with the concept of *tz'u*, which directs the subordinate
to give up direct invective for the indirect means of witty "artistry."
By the sixth century, the graph for *feng* took on a "speech" radical

to distinguish it from "wind" and was joined with that for *tz'u* to form a compound. Because of the essential identity of meaning, twentieth-century Chinese have used this compound as the equivalent of the Western word "satire"; modern translators have also not hesitated to render the graphs, either separately or in combination, as "satire."[37]

Like satire for John Dryden, *feng-tz'u* for the Chinese is considered a noble art, because its moral content places it in the mainstream of the Confucian tradition of literature as proponent of the Tao. And like Dryden, Liu Hsieh has taken the trouble to distinguish between the tradition of satire and its common offshoots of lampoon on the one hand, and pure humor (*hsieh*) and "enigma" (*yin*) on the other.

The mental processes of the people are as precipitous as mountains, and their mouths, when stopped, are like dammed-up rivers. As their resentment and anger differ, their expressions of these feelings in jests or derision also vary. When once long ago Hua Yuan left his armor on the field after his defeat, those guarding the city ridiculed him in a song gibing at his protruding eyes. And when Tsang Ho lost his army, he was the subject of a tune referring to him as a dwarf. In both cases, the people mocked the appearance of the subjects of their songs in order to express their inner resentment and scorn. . . . Crude though these may be, inasmuch as they could be of service in the way of giving warning to people, they were all recorded in the *Book of Rites*. Thus we know that even humorous and enigmatic statements are not to be discarded.[38]

In Liu's view, therefore, the seeming lampoons of Hua Yuan and Tsang Ho are worthy to be included in the classics only because the scope of their attack extends beyond these individuals to a broader morality encompassing human society: (1) it expresses a legitimate public grievance, and (2) it "gives warning" to the people at large. Liu Hsieh may seem farfetched in his interpretation; but what is significant is the interpretation itself which reveals his understanding and acceptance of the *feng-tz'u* tradition. Humor and enigma, as pure forms of wit, are deemed unworthy of the designation "literature"; only when they are employed in the service of a general morality can they be considered worthy of preservation. As Liu writes in the verse summary ("encomium" or *tsan*) to his chapter, enigma and humor are merely the "straw and rush" (that is, offshoots) to the "silk and hemp" (or direct orthodoxy) of literature.

If their meshing with moral meaning is appropriate to
   the times,
They can be of great service to admonition [*feng*] and
   warning;
Should they meaninglessly toy with the comic,
They can prove greatly harmful to the spread of virtue.[39]

Dryden appears almost to be glossing these lines when he de-
nounces lampoon as that which unfairly destroys the reputations of
men, and justifiable only as revenge if the person attacked "is become a public nuisance. . . . 'Tis an action of virtue to make examples of vicious men. They may and ought to be upbraided . . . both
for their own amendment, if they are not yet incorrigible, and for
the terror of others. . . .[40]
   The common insistence of Liu and Dryden on morality of general
extension expressed in wit affirms the essential identity of *feng-tz'u*
and satire. Therefore, when Wu Ching-tzu took up his brush to
create the *Ju-lin wai-shih*, his own tradition directed him to combine his Confucian idealism (or morality) with humor and enigma (or
wit), and the result is a work of genuine satire.

VI Wu Ching–tzu's Satire

   Wu's Confucian ideals as they appear in his novel will constitute
the subject of the following chapter as a prelude to the full discussion of the origins and practice of our author's satirical techniques.
Before we venture into these subjects, however, we should solidify
the abstract ideas of our present discussion by examining one example of genuine satire from the *Ju-lin wai-shih*.
   In Chapter 3 of the novel, we encounter Fan Chin, a destitute
examination candidate who, having just become a provincial
graduate, is immediately lionized by Chang Ching-chai, a member
of the local gentry who provides him with a house, money, and
servants. Overexcited by all this good fortune, Fan's mother dies in
the beginning of Chapter 4, and Chang persuades Fan to pay a visit
to Tang Feng (T'ang Feng), Fan's examiner and magistrate of the
Kaoyao district in western Kwangtung province, in order to pressure him into making a contribution toward the expenses of the
funeral. When they see Tang, he is in the midst of trying to decide
the proper course of action concerning a bribe of fifty catties of beef
from Muslim elders who want him to ignore the emperor's recent

injunction against the slaughter of farm oxen. "Can I accept or not?" he asked of the wily Chang.

"I should say certainly not, sir," replied Chang. "You and I are officials and we only give our allegiance to the emperor, not to friends of the same faith. This reminds me of old Mr. Liu in the reign of Hung-wu. . . ."

"Which Mr. Liu?" asked the Magistrate.

"The one called Chi. He passed the Palace Examination in the third year of Hung-wu, placing fifth on the list."

"I thought he placed third," put in Fan Chin.

"No," Chang insisted. "Fifth. I read his examination papers. Later he entered the Han-lin Academy. One day Emperor Hung-wu went privately to his house, just like the emperor who visited [Chao] P'u one snowy night [*hsüeh-yeh fang P'u*]. But that same day, Prince Chang of Chiang-nan had sent him in a crock of pickled vegetables, and he opened it in the Emperor's presence, only to find that it was full of gold. The Emperor became very angry and said, 'He [the Prince] seems to think that everything in the world depends on you scholars!' The following day, he banished old Mr. Liu to the magistracy of Ch'ing-t'ien and then had him poisoned. Now how can you risk having the same thing happen to you?"

Since the Magistrate saw that Chang was simply overflowing with information, and moreover that what he was referring to was the actual history of the present dynasty, he could not but believe him. "How should I deal with the situation then?" he asked.[41]

The bad advice Chang gives in his answer eventually results in the death of one Muslim elder, an ensuing riot, and great disgrace for Magistrate Tang. But even before the detailing of these results, the text above already provides the reader with ample indication of the faultiness of the advice by satirizing the pedantry and stupidity of Chang and Fan, as well as the incompetence of the Magistrate who is too ignorant to question his advisor.

The critic who insists on considering only what Schorer calls the "achieved content" of this passage and who refuses to go outside of the text would not even be able to identify it as satire: internally, the passage gives no indication that it is anything but straightforward narrative. There is wit aplenty, but this wit is rhetorical and cannot be grasped apart from the given morality, immediately intelligible to Wu Ching-tzu's intended readers, with which it is inextricably interwoven.

We can assume that these readers would be familiar with all the topical facts, including the identities of Liu Chi and Chao P'u. The official *Ming History* (*Ming Shih*) records that Liu (1311–1375) was a native of Ch'ing-t'ien, one of the principal advisors of the first Ming emperor (Hung-wu), and highly instrumental in helping the latter overcome his rivals in his successful struggle to found the Ming empire. After the dynasty's establishment, Liu served as imperial historian before his retirement. His character is described as "stern" and "introverted." And although there is an indication that an enemy did try to poison him and eventually did cause him to become ill from "worry and anger," there is no real evidence that his death was due to anything but natural causes.[42] Chao P'u (921–991) lived two dynasties before Liu, but, according to the *Sung History* (*Sung Shih*), he was a similar sort of man in character (described as "profound and reticent of speech") and in historical significance, having helped the first Sung emperor establish his rule and earning the latter's high regard in the process. The incident of the pickles happened to him and not to Liu, though officially the crock was supposed to have contained "sea delicacies" (*hai-wu*) and not pickled vegetables (*hsiao-ts'ai*). Moreover, the Sung emperor was not angry, but permitted him to keep the gift.[43]

These facts of Chinese history are intrinsically relevant to the satirical meaning of our passage. For it is only against these facts that the general morality—the protest against the civil-service examination system of the time—can be properly understood; and it is in the course of this understanding that the satirical art of the passage also reveals itself. So let us examine the text in light of these facts.

First, the *Ju-lin wai-shih*'s theme of satirizing the examination system is sounded by Chang's seeming recall of the exact date of Liu Chi's passing of the palace examination as well as Liu's exact place on the list, thus indicating his true concerns, when in actuality Liu was already a high official at the founding of the Ming. Fan Chin's interruption shows his own ignorance and pedantry, and Chang's insistence that Liu did place fifth indicates further Chang's arrogant stupidity and dishonesty, as it is clear he could neither have read Liu's nonexistent examination essay nor known of any entrance into the Han-lin Academy. Second Chang's confusion of Liu and Chao P'u is psychologically set up when he employs the phrase *hsüeh-yeh fang P'u* ("snowy night visit P'u") to describe Liu's situation, indicating that he vaguely recalls Chao P'u's story. The fuzziness and vulgarity of Chang's memory is further revealed by his subsequent substitution of "pickled vegetables" for the more elegant "sea delicacies." Finally, the falseness of Chang's account of the emperor's reaction to the crock of gold is accentuated by Chang's contention that Liu was banished to Ch'ing-t'ien. Ch'ing-t'ien was Liu's native home, and it is simply absurd for any official to be banished to the magistracy of his hometown. The obvious suggestion is that Chang vaguely connects Ch'ing-t'ien with Liu and blurts it out here in an erroneous context. The poisoning story gives further evidence of Chang's defective memory and learning, indicating that he does not even know the original story of Chao P'u, since the gold-crock incident is recorded to show the Sung emperor's trust and respect for Chao and not his ire.

All this confusion makes it evident that Chang does not purposely make up his story, which would have been bad enough. As the object of the author's satire, he is not even accorded the credit of a fabricating intelligence, but is destroyed by being made to reveal an utter stupidity punctuated by pedantic arrogance. The point does not stop here, however. Chang Ching-chai is not a particularized hero like, for example, Captain Ahab, who himself embodies a large measure of the self-contained morality in *Moby Dick*. If the morality of the *Ju-lin wai-shih* stops with Chang, he would be no more than a comical character. But Chang in no way dominates the novel as Ahab does *Moby Dick*: the author soon leaves him to go on to many other examples of idiocy, dishonesty, and pedantry. From the panorama of all the characters of the *Ju-lin wai-shih*, the more universal morality of satire reveals itself: the satirist is not attacking Chang so much as the corrupting and demeaning Chinese examination system of the time which produces and nurtures such dolts as Chang and Fan and Magistrate Tang. This moral attack, moreover, is meaningful to the novel's Ch'ing dynasty readers because, even for those who succeeded, the system is, in a real sense, the bane of their existence.

VII *Satire and the Novel*

The foregoing should have made clear that, because of its rhetorical character, satirical art differs fundamentally from art of a more purely expressive nature. While the *Ju-lin wai-shih* unquestionably exhibits a close-knit characterization and a narrative tone of detachment and restraint, it would be misleading to directly apply to it standards and criteria gleaned from realistic fiction. Whatever else it may resemble, the *Ju-lin wai-shih* is most basically satire; and it is as satire that its artistic merit should be measured.

The concept of fiction today is, by and large, tied in with the concept of the novel and, if we were to accept Ian Watt's conclusions, the Western novel is formalistically connected with realism. As Watt explains, realism in the novel has as a "primary criterion" the truth of individual experience—"individual experience which is always unique and therefore new."[44] In contrast, satirical truth is by nature social and general, written not so much to express the author's personal vision as to mesh with the reader's experience and thereby to gain his assent. It is likely for this reason that Defoe, Richardson, and Fielding, who pioneered realism in fiction, and not Jonathan Swift, who concentrated on satire, are considered to be the fathers of the English novel. For while *Moll Flanders* or *Pamela* or *Tom Jones* are unquestionably designated as novels, most critics would not put *Gulliver's Travels* in that category.[45] As Northrup Frye observes, satire deals less with people than with stereotyped mental attitudes and thus differs from the novel in its characterization, "which is stylized rather than naturalistic, and presents people [only] as mouthpieces of the ideas they represent."[46] To say that we shall judge the *Ju-lin wai-shih* primarily as a work of satire is to caution ourselves against the unreflective application of novelistic criteria—of internal, psychological characterization, of a unified plot structure, for example—in our judgment, as have so many critics of the past. R. C. Elliott's remarks on the question of the criticism of satirical fiction certainly holds true, *mutatis mutandis*, for the *Ju-lin wai-shih:*

We are all novel-centered, I suspect, in our dealings with fiction of every kind; it is a difficult orientation to overcome. Still, our expectations when we read Petronius or *Candide* are by no means the same as when we read George Eliot. It would be absurd to criticize Lucian's *True Story* because "Lucian" (the "I" of the narrative) does not grow into a rounded character. It is the nature of the enterprise that he shall remain the same stolid, deadpan recorder to incredible adventures.[47]

In light of all this, we can see that it is probably a misnomer to call the *Ju-lin wai-shih* a "novel." I continue to do so in this study because I do not wish to depart from a designation of long-standing and feel moreover that the term itself should be expanded from its provincial eighteenth-century meaning to include under it all long narratives of a fictional nature. By using it in connection with the *Ju-lin wai-shih*, on the other hand, I do not mean to imply that the work necessarily contains formal characteristics in common with the early European works which beat that popular designation.

With all this said, we can at last proceed to the examination of the moral basis of the satire in the *Ju-lin wai-shih*.

CHAPTER 3

Morality: The Eremitic Ideal in the Ju-lin wai-shih

THE concept of satire presented in the preceding chapter, of an interacting unity between morality and wit, owes much to the studies of Alvin Kernan. But there is an important difference between Kernan's basic approach and the one used in this study. Anxious to preserve satire's "independence of artistic status," Kernan shies away from the discussion of topical issues to concentrate on satire's universal characteristics, its common manifestations of human "dullness." In stressing the sameness rather than the particular differences of satirical works, Kernan is able to remain largely within the confines of the text and rescue satire from what he considers to be its common confusion with history and biography.[1] But, as we have seen, the *Ju-lin wai-shih* is not comprehensible to us as satire without reading it in light of actual facts and factors not mentioned in the text, and we are led to the conclusion that, with some kinds of satire at least, art independent from history and biography is meaningless.

This is especially true of satire written in a context separated by time and culture from our own. Kernan can and does assume a common recognition of the moral meaning between the author and reader of the works he studies. Our analysis of a work of Ch'ing dynasty satire, on the other hand, presents a more fundamental problem of understanding not only for a modern Western student, but for present-day Chinese critics as well, largely because of the sweeping changes that have occurred in China over the last century and a half. Most published criticisms of the *Ju-lin wai-shih* discuss prominently the moral values in the work, and nearly everyone agrees that it sets out in some fashion to criticize the traditional examination system, as well as such social evils as false propriety, the unfair treatment of women, and superstition. Significant dispute, however, continues over the moral or philosophical standards against which Wu Ching-tzu measures the literati society, and it is this dispute which clouds the overall understanding and evaluation of Wu's art. I can think of at least three specific reasons why the *Ju-lin wai-shih* has been so often misunderstood in our times, and I shall list them in an inverse order of importance.

I Difficulties of Interpretation

The first of these reasons has to do with the uneven quality of some parts of the work, with the author's occasional loss of control. Wu Ching-tzu, in attempting to write sustained satire in a long, vernacular narrative, was setting out in a new direction, and we can understand his few lapses into pure comedy and invective. It is also characteristic of the pioneer to grope about, sometimes mistakenly, for bits and pieces of tradition to follow. We thus find him copying in part the structure of the *Water Margin (Shui-hu chuan)*, an earlier novel of a vastly different character; and C. T. Hsia is certainly right in his assertion that careful study of the sources of many of the anecdotes in the *Ju-lin wai-shih* would reveal Wu's free and sometimes forced adoption of jokes and stories popular among the literati circles of his time.[2] Add to all this the distinct possibility of later interpolations in the extant text, and we can see why modern critics are hard put to explain away all seeming inconsistencies and disparities under a unified scheme. I hasten to add, on the other hand, that we should not fall to the temptation of attributing all difficulties to the novel's unevenness; the bulk of it is well-crafted and thoroughly intelligible. Wu Ching-tzu's creative competence far outweighs his occasional lapses.

The second reason is tied to the internal character of the satire in the *Ju-lin wai-shih*. As we shall see later, Wu Ching-tzu chooses, as a rhetorical device, to modify the traditional mode of commentary by presenting his episodes with an objective pose, thus leaving the reader to draw his own conclusions. Given the unfamiliarity of most modern readers with the conditions satirized, these conclusions are not always obvious, and conflicting judgments are inevitable. Critics who focus on the novel's characterization, for example, are baffled at its lack of misanthropy, at the constant mixture of good and bad among so many characters. This mixture can make an accounting of the satirical point a formidable task.

These first two reasons partially explain the third and most important reason for the *Ju-lin wai-shih*'s many misinterpretations. Ever
since the early 1920s, critics have been eager to use the work to
further their own social causes. This attitude inevitably leads them
to approach the text with a priori needs and ideas and to interpret it
as relevant to their own situations, whether it indeed is or not.
Under the stress of different political needs, the *Ju-lin wai-shih* has
been seen to be nationalistic, or democratic, or pro women's rights,
and the work's essential conservatism is sidestepped or ignored altogether. Even today, few seem to bother to return to the cultural
and historical milieu in which the work was written in order objectively to ferret out its original moral meaning.

Even among those familiar with Chinese history and thought, this
moral meaning is far from obvious. The *Ju-lin wai-shih* apparently
criticizes the civil-service examination system, but some of its
"good" characters continue to participate; and a certain number of
officials are presented as both humane and intelligent. It seems to
point out the inhumanity of traditional propriety, but its moral centerpiece is an elaborate description of a rigidly formulated sacrificial
ceremony to a Confucian sage. It upholds the individuality of a
runaway concubine, but does not hesitate to train its sharpest barbs
on women, including one who is ridiculed for having large, unbound
feet. It resorts to invective in censuring the superstitious practices
of geomancy; yet it affirms the efficacy of the predictions of certain
fortune tellers and of dreams. Some of these seeming contradictions
may be explained as paradoxes; others can be put aside as inherent
defects, attributable to the author's inability to break cleanly from
the limits of his own history. But neither solution is satisfying. If the
Ju-lin wai-shih is true satire, its moral concern should be clear and
well-indicated throughout; it should not need to be salvaged by a
great deal of rationalization.

The major task of this chapter is to determine this moral concern,
now obscured by the cataclysmic changes of modern times, but
without which the satirical art of the *Ju-lin wai-shih* cannot be ascertained. The best way to do this is initially to examine two extremes
in the spectrum of interpretations of the novel's moral meaning. In
this way we shall be better able to arrive at a more balanced approach and lend a sharper accuracy to our judgment. These two
extremes consist of the Marxists, who bring to the scrutiny of the
Ju-lin wai-shih a set of externally formulated values and rules which

delimit (and sometimes even distort) the analysis of textual evidence; and, for want of a better term, the nihilists, who limit themselves to the internal confines of the text and are so baffled by its complexities that they conclude essentially that it espouses no discernible morality at all.[3]

II *The Marxist Interpretation*

The bulk of what I call the Marxist interpretation comes, as we might expect, from the People's Republic of China, beginning especially in 1954 when the Association of Chinese Authors (*Chung-kuo tso-chia hsieh-hui*) announced official encouragement and sanction for the study of the *Ju-lin wai-shih* with a convocation commemorating the bicentennial of Wu Ching-tzu's death. In the opening address, Mao Tun (Shen Yen-ping, b. 1896), then minister of culture, laid out the principles under which this effort was to proceed. He praised Wu Ching-tzu as a great writer because of his "realism" (*hsien-shih chu-yi*), his "merciless" exposé of "the corruption and stupidity of the feudalistic ruling class of his time," as well as his warm praise of " 'the little people' who came from the lower level of society and who were full of the spirit of resistance and creative talent." To Mao Tun, this realism represented "progressive thought" in the *Ju-lin wai-shih* and its "historical value," and critics were urged to examine the novel in terms of Wu's background and learning and the sociopolitical situation of his time.[4] While we cannot say that the many critics and scholars who took up Mao Tun's call and produced a mass of commentary on Wu Ching-tzu's satire are always in perfect agreement, this initial address seems already to have presented in outline form their common approach and thus defined the general area of their conclusions.

In his famous "Talks at the Yenan Forum on Literature and Art" of 1942, Mao Tse-tung had charged all Chinese critics to adopt a class approach to their evaluations of traditional literature. To Mao, the good Marxist critic must take a proletarian stand and must "distinguish among the literary and art works of past ages and determine . . . [his] attitude towards them only after examining their attitude to the people and whether or not they had any progressive significance historically." If they do not, the critic's duty is "to reject them," whatever their "artistic quality" in bourgeois terms.[5] Essentially Mao Tun and other Chinese critics of the *Ju-lin wai-shih* have adhered to these instructions, and the moral value they sought in the novel is none other than its "progressive significance" in the class-conscious Marxian scheme of human history. It is in these terms that the general Marxist conclusion that the *Ju-lin wai-shih* exhibits a praiseworthy degree of "realism" should be understood.[6]

This "realism" obviously refers to the "correct" grasp of the general truth of Marxian laws and not to the agnostic perceptions of fragmented truth basic to the realism which defines the modern Western novel. Marxist critics, in concluding that the *Ju-lin wai-shih* is an outstandingly realistic novel, are simply saying that the predominant part of its moral stance illustrates, ahead of its time, the oppressive evils of what they call the "feudalistic ruling class." To Ho Man-tzu, for example, Wu Ching-tzu's novel "tears off the masks from the faces of the representatives of the class enemies of the people and restores their ugly, ludicrous, and contemptible actual appearances."[7]

Others go even further in reading elements of a prescient Marxism into Wu Ching-tzu's moral position. To Wu Tsu-hsiang, our author shows in his novel nothing less than a "nationalistic spirit" as well as "hate and a feeling of rebellion" against "the foreign rule of the [Ch'ing dynasty] Manchus."[8] Hu Nien-yi does question this conclusion as "farfetched," but he goes on to praise Wu Ching-tzu for his "democratic" thought, which he sees as the motivating force behind Wu's satire.[9] Ho Ch'i-fang develops this idea further by noting Wu Ching-tzu's poverty as the condition which allowed him to become acquainted with "people from the lower social strata" and to admire their economic self-sufficiency.[10] And Wu Hsiao-ju even equates this latter point to a prophetic recognition of the Marxian labor theory of value: "I think that the most remarkable aspect of Wu Ching-tzu is his promotion of the idea of self-sufficiency, his high regard for the fruits of one's own labor. Because of this, he thus also indirectly opposes exploitation. This is also the primary key to what makes the *Ju-lin wai-shih* a product of realism."[11]

Such interpretations demonstrate the moralistic bent of Marxist criticism. In terms of the analysis of satire, the Marxist approach does show us the need for understanding satire's moral pole. In considering the *Ju-lin wai-shih*, however, Marxist critics start out with an a priori morality of their own, a "progressive realism" defined according to Marxian laws. They do not seek out the work's moral meaning in terms of its own historical or cultural context, but only in terms of how this meaning conforms or does not conform to predetermined values. It is not surprising, therefore, that Marxist criticism of the *Ju-lin wai-shih* shows itself to be predictable and limited, predictable because it must single out for praise only such elements as nationalism or democracy which conform to the Marxian scheme, and limited insofar as it cannot account for non-Marxian values in anything but negative terms. None of the many Marxist critics who have studied the *Ju-lin wai-shih* even bother to delineate systematically the Confucian thought that they admit is present, but remain content to relegate it to the general category of "feudalistic" elements. Ho Ch'i-fang, for example, realizes that the kind of Confucian eremitism the character Wang Mien exemplifies in Chapter 1 has a long history in Chinese society; yet he does not consider the particulars of this branch of Confucian thought, which would clearly add insight into the novel's moral stance; instead, he is satisfied to say, along with others, that many of Wu Ching-tzu's ideals are "conservative" and "not admirable." The *Ju-lin wai-shih* may exhibit an intelligible moral scheme, but if part or all of this scheme espouses values denied by the Marxian system, Marxist criticism will not be equal to the task of describing it.

III   *The Nihilist Interpretation*

In the sense that the Marxist critic misses the mark because of his slighting of textual evidence and his overreliance on external values and laws, the nihilist is opposite to him, since he ignores outside information and is thus unable to arrive at a satisfactory explanation of the internal contents of the text. Though relatively few critics of the *Ju-lin wai-shih* can be called nihilist without qualification, the conclusion that the work presents no positive values is important, because it is one extreme result of an approach to the criticism of fiction that is current in the West and because non-Marxist critics of the *Ju-lin wai-shih* have a tendency to include elements of this view in their analyses of the work's moral values.

The nihilists' careful focus on the text itself does yield the important insight that the satirist in the *Ju-lin wai-shih* nearly always maintains a certain distance from his characters, a distance which casts doubt on the simple conclusion that the novel espouses a clear and consistent moral concern. Many critics who come to this conclusion nevertheless attempt in some fashion to tie together the many episodes to some sort of philosophical system and, in that sense, cannot really be called nihilist. It is highly significant, however, that a few have read the interior chapters of the novel very closely and, bothered by the mixture of "good" and "bad" in the majority of characters, have concluded that it essentially does little more than poke fun at the faults and foibles of Chinese literati society, and that moreover it does so from an uncommitted and noncondemning point of view.

Ogawa Tamaki, a genuine pioneer in the criticism of the *Ju-lin wai-shih*, takes the first step on the nihilistic path by questioning, quite validly, the critical habit of equating the events of the novel with actual history. "To me," he writes in 1933, "while one can see a probable aspect of the times according to things described in the *Ju-lin wai-shih*, one definitely cannot take everything written there as facts or demonstrations of events which actually occurred. . . . This is, after all, a work of fiction."

This line of thinking, by clearly separating fiction from actuality, leads Ogawa to de-emphasize questions of moral relevance in the search for the meaning of the *Ju-lin wai-shih*. He goes on to state that "Rather than say that it simply opposes action and thought which are entrapped within propriety, habit, etc., [I would prefer to say that] perhaps the one special feature of the entire work is that it approaches everything with an emotion of tenderness."[12] Ogawa does not directly deny that the novel contains positive moral value; but these observations are the first which play down the novel's moral commitment as the primary feature. To Ogawa, Wu Ching-tzu probably wrote his novel only as a sort of "leisurely amusement" and, at any rate, "did not commit himself to the extent of definitely destroying the bad characters or causing the good characters to prosper. He probably did not even intend to distort facts in order to make [the reader] follow his beliefs."[13]

There is only a short distance from such a conclusion to one which denies all positive morality in the *Ju-lin wai-shih*. Inada Takashi, who has made a complete Japanese translation of the work, does make this final leap in an article published in 1962, some thirty years after Ogawa's.[14] Writing largely in reaction to Marxist criticism of the *Ju-lin wai-shih*, Inada reexamines with great care the accounts of the sacrificial ceremonies at T'ai-po (Chapter 37), as well as portrayals of such major "positive" *(koteiteki)* characters as Dr. Yu (Yü Yü-te), Chuang Shao-kuang, and Tu Shao-ching (Tu Shao-ch'ing). He notes that the T'ai-po (Tai Po in *The Scholars*) rituals represent the one great symbolic, positive moral act in the novel. Yet these rituals are recounted in a technical, mechanical fashion tedious to the reader but acted out by those involved with a seriousness that approaches the comical. Thus, while the author's attitude toward the whole affair may seem to be revealed by the exclamation of the onlookers that they have never seen such an uplifting and marvelous display, could it be, Inada asks, that Wu Ching-tzu is merely making them express the shallow enthusiasm of tourists? For, after all, the novel later shows that the lofty moral intentions of the instigators—to teach the people the practice of ancient ceremonies and music in order to produce human talent—never come to pass. In Chapter 55, the shrine falls into utter disrepair, its message long forgotten.

All this, to Inada, can only cast doubt on the author's moral purpose. "To the author Wu Ching-tzu," Inada asks, "were the sacrifices at the T'ai-po shrine finally a matter made positive as the outstanding act of the age? When the author took up the pen regarding the sacrifices, did he really approach the matter as a necessarily positive act?"[15] More probably, he goes on to suggest, the account is no more than a rendering of a wishful fantasy, a fantasy contrasted with the emptiness of the actual world. Far from presenting a positive morality, "the author . . . was looking at the Quixotic manner of ancient ceremonies and ancient music" as well as "the Quixotic ways of himself."[16] For many of the participants, including the one patterned after the author himself (Tu Shao-ching), are not really shown to be paragons of virtue but exhibit the same foibles as others satirized throughout the *Ju-lin wai-shih*.

Inada continues this line of argument in his examination of various "so-called positive characters" of the novel. He sees "the spirit of independence (or pride) of each individual" and the longing for a society of "trust and sympathy" as the moral motivation behind the portrayal of Dr. Yü; but, without looking into what Confucianism is, he concludes that this kind of morality "belongs to a different category than Confucianism."[17] Chuang Shao-kuang, on the other hand, appears too idealistically presented to Inada to be taken seriously. For Chuang is not one involved in any way with the common man; instead, he is invited to advise the emperor and is privileged to retire in comfort to an island set physically and symbolically apart from the world, in distinct contrast to all the other characters who must continue to struggle for their material needs. Chuang, as Inada puts it, is the author's great "lie," and is too much of a fantasy to embody any positive moral significance.[18] As for Tu Shao-ching, it seems clear to Inada that the author regards him as "absurd," as a character whose foibles are the author's own, revealed like a self-confession through the mouths of various internal critics. Even though Tu does draw praise from some, Inada concludes that his portrait is also Quixotic, reflecting the moral absurdity of the human condition.[19]

In contrast to these so-called positive characters whose descriptions exhibit so little actual morality, Inada find those characters with moral flaws to be the most impressive. Like Ogawa, he stresses the view that Wu Ching-tzu's "negative" characters are generally not contemptible: "Rather, I feel an unlimited love for them. If there is no strong human interest and sympathy for the author's so-called negative characters, this kind of feeling cannot come about."[20]

Inada's general argument is that, contrary to those who hold that Wu Ching-tzu advocates positive moral values in his satire, the Ju-lin wai-shih neither contains discernible moral standards nor criticizes social ills with consistency and vigor and, instead, portrays nothing beyond human absurdity. While the novel is non-Marxist in its moral stance, it is also non-Confucian: whatever morality it demonstrates is tied in with a reality of life too complex to be explained under any one philosophical system. "The so-called positive characters . . .," Inada concludes, "are definitely not the formulated products of a single important element and [their moral meaning] cannot be grasped from a single point of view. Consequently, the word 'positive' must usually need qualification." For Wu Ching-tzu appears to neither affirm nor deny the literati he describes, and is seemingly content to show the comedy or irony of their world, an empty world where, in Inada's words, "If there is no correctness, there is also no incorrectness."

For the very reason Inada's views appear extreme, he becomes the ideal spokesman for the nihilistic tendency in the interpretation of the Ju-lin wai-shih. While no other critic so completely denies the existence of a comprehensible system of moralistic thought in the novel, Inada's conclusions are similar to those of certain non-Marxist critics sensitive enough to perceive the novel's bewildering mixture of vice and virtue. Yüeh Heng-chün, for example, writes in a recent article from Taiwan that all the characters in the Ju-lin wai-shih lead "wasteful" and "useless" lives, "meaninglessly" moved about by the tides of fortune. Moreover, Yüeh charges that the author, by not directly providing any explanation for the reader, allows whatever lessons these lives may give to remain hidden: "The work as a whole really lacks psychological revelations and internal explanation."[21]

Such observations present a challenge to our premise that the *Ju-lin wai-shih* contains genuine satire. For, in the absence of a moral purpose, the novel may be seen to present human society as amusing or absurd, but definitely not in need of censure. The only valid rebuttle of these nihilist conclusions is to discover the "internal explanation" nihilist critics cannot find, aided by external information they do not consider. For, even for the nihilists themselves, the lack of an answer to the meaning of their subject is not altogether satisfactory. Inada admits that he cannot say with certainty that orthodox Confucian thought "did not rest" in Wu Ching-tzu's "inner mind"; for Yüeh, the lives of the novel's literati appear meaningless only because the author fails to provide a direct explanation.[22]

Actually, Wu Ching-tzu does take pains to provide such an explanation by sandwiching the rest of his novel between clearly idealized accounts of the recluse-artist Wang Mien in the opening chapter and of individuals we shall call "the four eccentrics" in Chapter 55. These are the moral paragons who, by the example of their lives, unequivocally show the positive morality of the *Ju-lin wai-shih*. Despite their announced search for an internal explanation of the novel's moral stance, neither Inada nor Yüeh bothers to account for these key characters. Wang Mien and the four eccentrics, however, do not demonstrate a morality and a philosophy easily grasped in the popular understanding of Confucianism; like Wu Ching-tzu in real life, they choose to retire to their own worlds rather than to take up the stereotyped Confucian injunction to actively serve society. Yet, like their creator Wu Ching-tzu, they exhibit a Confucianist purpose and temperate approach to life quite distinct from Taoists who renounce all worldly values as relative. Since the Confucianism they dislpay is not of the ordinary variety, we would do well to consult relevant studies of lesser-known aspects of Confucian thought in order to fathom their meaning and their import.

IV *The Eremitic Ideal*

Confucianism in traditional China was never a one-dimensional moral and philosophical system which simply sanctioned and demanded service to state and society. In his study of Confucian "Conventions of Protest," David Nivison finds that while Confucianism justified the civil-service examination system as the "hallmark" of the state and the vehicle by which one fulfilled one's "basic duty to family and to the world,"

Yet almost from the beginning of this institution in the later empire, the examinations, and the educational standards they produced, were resented and criticized. . . . This polyphony of protest may be found in every generation. And the surprising fact is that throughout all this we find the examination-education complex, the function and effect of which was to ensure the dominance of the Confucian classical tradition, criticized precisely by appeal to *Confucian* moral, aesthetic, and political values.[23]

This protest shows what Nivison calls the "idealistic side" of Confucianism, a side no less important than the more pragmatic one shown by those who participated in the affairs of society.[24] This idealistic side adheres closely to the pure cultivation of the Confucian virtues of *jen* ("benevolence"), *yi* ("righteousness"), and *hsiao* ("filial piety"); to what has been called the "amateur ideal" in the pursuit of learning and the development of talent;[25] and to those parts of the Confucian canon which, as F. W. Mote has explained, stress that "a man should serve when he could maintain and actively promote his principles, and that he should withdraw when the conditions of public service were degrading, or when his principles were threatened."[26] The existence of such ideals under the Confucian umbrella shows, as Nivison suggests, that Confucianism should better be looked upon as a complex system of tensions which was itself the source of internal disputes and opposing manifestations. It is in this light that the morality of the *Ju-lin wai-shih,* a morality of protest, becomes most intelligible.

Apart from Marxist "progressive realism" or nihilist "absurdity," satire in the *Ju-lin wai-shih* manifests a morality clearly compatible with the Confucian ideology of protest. To comprehend this morality, we should first consider the novel's true paragons, Wang Mien and the four eccentrics, by means of whom the author specifically lays out the moral standards against which he measures the plethora of characters in the rest of his work.[27]

That Wang Mien and the four eccentrics are intended to represent a clear contrast to their more mundane compatriots is evident in their respective introductions in the novel.[28] The chapter on Wang begins with a traditional lyric and comment decrying the incorrigible greed of "people in the world" for "riches, rank, success, and fame"; but, the narrator goes on, "there once appeared an outstandingly great person" whose name was Wang Mien.[29] This type of introduction is repeated in the chapter dealing with the four eccentrics, who are said to appear "among the townfolk" just as true learning and true humanity were disappearing from society.[30] Unlike all other characters in the novel, therefore, Wang Mien and the eccentrics are presented as elite figures, standing morally and intellectually above the rest of society. As such, they cannot be objects of satire. On the contrary, we are practically told to regard them as exemplars of the novel's moral ideals, ideals violated in one way or another by the multitude of dunces who troop across the pages of the *Ju-lin wai-shih*. To comprehend these ideals, therefore, we must look for the moral constant in these five individuals.

This moral constant is made fairly clear. Wang Mien and the eccentrics display a great many similarities. All of them are superior men, morally and intellectually above their social acquaintances who usually fail to understand their motives. Primarily, all of them adhere to a life of withdrawal and self-cultivation which corresponds exactly to what Mote calls "voluntary eremitism," an aspect of Confucianism which stresses its "idealistic side" and which, as Mote affirms, is as "equally valid" a manifestation of Confucian thought as the more commonly perceived idea of social participation and public service.[31]

A Confucian eremite, according to Mote, is one who is most clearly identified by his "renunciation of office holding." The term *yin-yi* or "recluse" in traditional Chinese society

signified withdrawal from the active public life in the service of society that Confucian ethics prescribed as the most suitable course for all those whose abilities, cultivation, and learning qualified them for it. To bar one's gates and earn one's own living without reliance on the emolument of office, to display a lack of regard for the social status which could be attained only by entering officialdom, and to devote one's life to self-cultivation, scholarship or artistic pursuits made one a recluse. By the mores of Confucian society, this was a step which set one apart, which justified the special appellation.[32]

We can see that this is an exact description of Wang Mien and the eccentrics, all of whom possess superior ability, and all of whom bar

their gates in open contempt for the advantages of officialdom. It is
in terms of this definition that the seemingly bizarre behavior of all
of them can be understood and appreciated.

V Wang Mien as Eremite

In the *Ju-lin wai-shih*'s account of Wang Mien, we are told that,
while tending a water buffalo, he overhears four strangers picnick-
ing under a willow after a sudden shower. Oblivious of the natural
beauty of their surroundings, these four center their conversation
around Wei Su, a gentry member and the most prominent man in
the district, in evident admiration of his wealth and status. Wei is
said to have just purchased a new house larger than the one he
occupied in the capital and worth two thousand taels of silver. Local
officials, including the district magistrate, are said to have gathered
there to pay their respects at the housewarming.

"The magistrate is a Metropolitan Graduate in the year *jen-wu* and a student of Mr. Wei," said the thin man. "It was only right for him to pay his
respects."
"My son-in-law's father is also a pupil of Mr. Wei," said the fat man. "He
has a post as a magistrate now in Honan Province. The day before yester-
day, my son-in-law came to visit me, bringing two catties of dried veni-
son—that's it on this dish. When he goes back, he's going to ask his father to
write a letter of introduction so that I can call on Mr. Wei. Then, if Mr. Wei
condescends to come to the village to return the visit, the villagers won't
dare to turn their donkeys and pigs loose to eat grain in my fields any
more."
"Mr. Wei is a real scholar," said the thin man.
"Recently when he left the capital," said the man with the beard, "I heard
the emperor himself escorted him out of the city, taking his hand and
walking over ten steps with him. It was only after Mr. Wei had repeatedly
bowed and entreated him to go no further that the emperor got into his
palanquin and left. Judging by this, Mr. Wei will probably soon become a
great official."[33]

The narrator relates, without comment, that Wang Mien, who
heretofore has continued to read books obtained from a vendor at
the village school, stops his reading and concentrates on his painting. It may be somewhat extreme to take this conversation as the
only cause of Wang's decision to withdraw to the cultivation of his
special talent, but the passage does indicate aspects of official life—
the obsequious admiration of possessors of status and wealth, the

bullying tendencies of those in power, the competitive bragging—which repulse him. When Wei Su takes a liking to Wang's paintings and indicates to the magistrate that he wants to meet Wang, the latter, to the consternation of his kindly neighbor Old Chin (Ch'in Lao), refuses to accept the invitation. "If the magistrate sends an invitation, he must mean well," said the perplexed old man. "So why not go? The proverb says, 'Magistrates can ruin families.' Why ask for trouble?"

Old Chin is no more than the average, practical man, unable to comprehend the higher principle of Wang's reply: "You heard what I've been saying. Don't you see the point of the stories of Tuan-kan Mu and Hsieh Liu? I definitely don't want to go."[34] Tuan-kan Mu and Hsieh Liu are mentioned together in the *Mencius* as examples of ancient worthies who refused to see a feudal lord because they held no office in his jurisdiction.[35] In this particular reference, Mencius holds that Tuan-kan, who avoided a meeting by climbing over a wall, and Hsieh, who bolted his door, probably went too far and that, "when forced," it is all right to answer such a summons. Nevertheless, the point is made that a truly "worthy" *(hsien)* person treasures the preservation of his principles over what he sees as demeaning obeisance to those in power.[36] In thus placing Wang Mien in the company of well-known exemplars of Confucian eremitism, Wu Ching-tzu is clearly advocating those values associated with a Confucian recluse. It is therefore natural that Wang Mien later deliberately stays away when the magistrate comes personally to his door, and then even runs off to another town in order to escape reprisal. For Wang, as the narrator explicitly states, is no ordinary man; "While not seeking any office, he did not even associate with friends, spending his days behind closed doors."[37] Eventually, he lives out his life

as a hermit in the K'uai-chi Mountains, and never disclosed his real name. When later he fell ill and died, his neighbors there collected some money and buried him at the foot of the mountain. . . . Ludicrously enough, when writers and scholars nowadays refer to Wang Mien, they all call him Wang, the Commissioner of Records. Actually, how can one say that Wang Mien was an official for even a single day? Thus [to correct this error] I have tried to make clear [his real biography].[38]

In this last comment, we can see Wu Ching-tzu's penchant for irony coming to the fore: common men, dunces that they are, are able to

honor Wang only by an official title, not knowing that they thus
destroy the very reason for his greatness!

VI *The Four Eccentrics*

The *Ju-lin wai-shih*'s account of the four eccentrics in Chapter 55
is far less detailed than that of Wang Mien; but is it clear that the
behavior of these colorful men reflects the same moral ideals of
Confucian eremitism so fully propounded in Wang's fictionalized
biography. Unlike the Taoist recluses to whom they are likened by
certain commentators, these four men neither completely cut themselves off from their fellow men nor engage in aimless self-in-
dulgence. The Confucian recluse, as Mote describes him, "might
indeed be somewhat eccentric, or he might be simply what we call a
retired gentleman of leisure, perhaps even one of great means living
in elegant fashion. More often he was a man of modest means, living
by teaching or working his own land, or a scholar living in poverty. .
. . the serious life is not demanded of him."[39]
Thus, just as Wang Mien makes a simple living by selling his own
paintings, Chi Hsia-nien, the calligrapher who "from his youth had
neither family nor job," lives frugally in a monastery, earning
enough for his board by his art and giving what is left of his funds "to
any poor man he happened to meet."[40] Wang Tai (Wang T'ai), the
master of *wei-ch'i* (a "chess" game better known in modern times by
the Japanese word *go*), sells spills for a livelihood; Kai Kuan (Kai
K'uan) the painter, once a rich pawnbroker, expresses no regrets for
the fortune he lost and lives cheerfully in a dingy teashop where he
earns an income of "fifty or sixty coppers" a day, barely enough to
"keep him in fuel and rice"; in the end, he accepts a post as a tutor at
a salary of eight taels.[41] And Ching Yuan (Ching Yüan) the musician
is happy with his profession as a tailor, declaring "Now everyday I
earn six or seven cents, and after I've eaten my fill, whether I want
to strum my lyre or do some calligraphy, it's all up to me. I neither
yearn for the riches or status of others nor wait upon anyone's pleasure, accountable neither to those above nor those below. Isn't it
pleasant?"[42]
It is thus clear that contentment with the simple life is what frees
these paragons to pursue higher things, the cultivation of personal

dignity and genuine virtue on the one hand, and the full development of natural talent on the other. Released from the necessity of
having to compromise his ideals of personal perfection for practical
reasons, Chi Hsia-nien is able to demand three days' preparation
every time he does his calligraphy, to use only a certain kind of
brush, to require that three or four persons hold down his paper
properly, and to write only when he happens to be in the mood. In
this way, it is easy to understand that he can reach the limits of his
potential and excel. For all these paragons, the development of
talent is pursued for its own sake, not for any utilitarian or profes-
sional motive, and their achievements would naturally be superior.
Wang Tai, who plays *wei-ch'i* for the love of the game, thus wins
easily over another who plays for money and reputation. Wang's
exclamation, after playing a masterful game, that "I am so extremely
happy that I don't need wine," also explains the reason for his
success. [43]

By design, the four eccentrics reach the highest plateau of excel-
lence in the four leisurely pursuits of the Confucian gentleman:
music, chess, calligraphy, and painting. To the Confucian, this development of natural ability is only possible for those who possess
altruistic virtue, which directs a man to turn aside utilitarian enticements for the uncompromising pursuit of perfection. Accomplished talent is thus also a sign of moral worth. As men of such
accomplished talent, Wang Mien and the four eccentrics are therefore truly superior beings, in no way less superior even than the
ruler whom they might have served. As Mencius quotes the Confucian disciple Tseng Tzu to justify his own refusal of a prince's summons, in a passage Mote also cites, "The wealth of [the kingdoms of]
Chin and Ch'u cannot be rivalled. They may have their wealth, but I
have my benevolence; they may have their exalted rank, but I have
my integrity. In what way do I suffer by comparison?" [44]

VII   *The Truly Superior Man*

It follows therefore that the truly superior man does not go to the
prince, who must rather come to him as a student to his teacher.
"When a Commoner is summoned to corvée," Wan Chang argues in
another part of the *Mencius*, "he goes to serve. Why then should he
refuse to go when he is summoned to an audience?"
Mencius' reasoning is to the point:

"It is right for him to go and serve, but it is not right for him to present himself. Moreover, for what reason does the prince wish to see him?"

"For the reason that he is well-informed and that he is good and wise."

"If it is for the reason that he is well-informed, even the Emperor does not summon his teacher, let alone a feudal lord. If it is for the reason that he is a good and wise man, then I have never heard of summoning such a man when one wishes to see him."[45]

It is in light of this Mencian argument that the account of the first Ming emperor's visit to Wang Mien can be understood. For unlike the magistrate who haughtily invites Wang via a messenger, the emperor-to-be comes personally, like a proper Confucian prince, calling himself "a rough and ready fellow" and begging in the humblest terms for Wang's advice. What Wang has to say on the occasion is also typically Confucian: "If you use benevolence and righteousness to win the people, who would not follow you? But if you use military might to subjugate them. . . . I'm afraid their righteousness would not bear the shame of submission."[46]

For Wang Mien and the four eccentrics, this true superiority, recognized and honored by princes, is tied completely to their eremitism. They are the genuine paragons of the *Ju-lin wai-shih* because they steadfastly separate themselves from the common striving for wealth and status. They are clearly intended to stand in contrast to the host of dunces who inhabit the satirical world of the *Ju-lin wai-shih*, men and women who demonstrate in example after example the demeaning role those must accept who follow the competitive path to practical gain.

The early Hsien-chai lao-jen ("Old Man of the Studio of Leisure") preface, attached to the earliest extant (1803) edition of the *Ju-lin wai-shih*, makes the following important remarks:

This book as a whole takes career, fame, wealth, and rank [*kung-ming fu-kuei*] as its theme. There are those who are tempted by *kung-ming fu-kuei* and either play up to people or look down on people; those who, relying on *kung-ming fu-kuei*, brag to other people; those who pretend not to be interested in *kung-ming fu-kuei* and consider themselves superior, only to be seen through and laughed at by people. Ultimately, the book regards the level of those who reject *kung-ming fu-kuei* as the highest, like the rock which stands against the current.[47]

The paragons we have been discussing, along with a few others like Dr. Yu, Chuang Shao-kuang, and Tu Shao-ching, can be collectively seen as this rock; most of the *Ju-lin wai-shih*, however, is taken up with accounts of the current, which represents society gone mad in the quest for *kung-ming fu-kuei*, the general object of Wu Ching-tzu's satire.

VIII *The* Kung-ming fu-kuei *Factor*

To look at the *Ju-lin wai-shih* in this way can solve many of the puzzles connected with the ultimate moral position of the work, puzzles solved by neither the Marxists nor the nihilists. From considering the accounts of Wang Mien and the four eccentrics, the obvious moral indicators of the novel, we can see the essential irrelevance of the "progressive realism" the Marxists seek. For, far from negating "feudalistic" thought, the novel's ideology centers around the emphatic affirmation of the idealistic side of orthodox Confucianism. Wu Ching-tzu does attack certain institutions of his society, but he does so from clearly reactionary and not progressive standards, defending and appealing to Confucian values in a time-honored fashion. It is therefore inaccurate and misleading to attribute to his work such unlikely features as nationalism or democracy as understood by modern Marxism. The *Ju-lin wai-shih* not only preaches against service to the *Manchu* government, but to *all* governments whose terms are seen inevitably to threaten uncompromising adherence to Confucian ideals. Nor does it really advocate the cause of "the little people" as a social class. In the novel's scale of inferior and superior, socioeconomic status itself is not a fundamental factor: rich or poor, famous or obscure, a man is superior if he sees through and rejects *kung-ming fu-kuei* and decidedly inferior if he proves willing to compromise his integrity in its pursuit. Shen Big Foot (Shen Ta-chiao), the go-between, and Pin-niang (P'in-niang), the courtesan, are both bonafide members of the proletariat, but neither can qualify as a superior person. Chuang Shao-kuang and Dr. Yu, by contrast, can clearly be called members of the feudalistic ruling class, but no one will deny that they are among the most morally upright and admirable of Wu Ching-tzu's characters. If Wu does tend to stress the poverty of his paragons, it is because he is also stressing their unwillingness to give up their independent self-cultivation for the sake of wealth and luxury. The rich (Chuang Shao-kuang is one case) are not necessarily censored, just as the poor (who make up a large part of the population of dunces in the novel) are not always praised. Our satirist-author was clearly more concerned that the rich not allow their wealth to get in the way of their benevolence and righteousness, and that the poor not join in the competition for wealth and status and put aside their moral and intellectual development along the way.

Just as the quest for *kung-ming fu-kuei* transcends social classes, as the one ultimate and unqualified evil in the *Ju-lin wai-shih*, it also transcends individual persons. In terms of understanding the *Ju-lin wai-shih*, this is an extremely important point, one missed by the nihilists and others who set out to classify all characters into rigid categories of good and bad. For, as the nihilists soon become aware, few characters in the novel represent either pure goodness or pure evil, and the mixture of virtue and vice can leave the reader confused and bewildered as to the author's actual sympathies. Even aside from those major "so-called positive" characters Inada discusses, we can readily cite such examples as Ma Chun-shang (Ma Ch'un-shang), who commits himself completely and stubbornly to the examination system but who retains enough righteousness and benevolence to spend unhesitatingly his entire savings to rescue a friend from the authorities (Chapter 14); or Yu Yu-ta (Yü Yu-ta), described as a man of rare character and learning, who nevertheless participates in a corrupt scheme to free a murderer for money (Chapter 44); or Pan Number Three (P'an San), a gangster boss and perpetrator of a long list of crimes who nevertheless treats Kuang Chao-jen with genuine kindness and generosity (Chapter 19). The first step in the solution of these difficulties involves the realization that the satirist is not really extolling any other virtues than those of the eremitic and, conversely, not criticizing any other vices than those connected with the blind quest for *kung-ming fu-kuei*.

Characters in the *Ju-lin wai-shih* are not depicted as innate dunces, but rather as people whose original (good) natures become ruined partly or wholly by a social system which directs them to take the wrong means to the wrong ends. Ma or Yu or Pan or, especially, Kuang are not praised or satirized ultimately for their honesty or cunning, but really only for whether the quest for *kung-ming fu-kuei* represents their primary direction in life. Except for the paragons, few completely escape the poison of this quest; but neither is everyone so besmirched as to lose all goodness and all humanity. Most simply drift about, unable to overcome the tremendous barrier *kung-ming fu-kuei* presents to the attainment of true virtue and true learning.

By focusing his criticism upon an aberrant social situation rather than upon any individual, Wu Ching-tzu is again consistent with Confucian doctrine which has always affirmed the fundamental goodness of human nature. The absence of misanthropy is the one significant difference between Wu's satire and that of many of his Western counterparts. In my opinion, it is for this reason that Wu can and does inject so much realism into a mode of literature that, to fulfill its rhetorical mission, is known to regularly exaggerate and simplify. For the view that man is not innately ignorant or evil but only occasionally becomes so allows for a more objective portrayal of human character and behavior. Wu Ching-tzu, as Ogawa and Inada testify, is really a tenderhearted satirist who accepts the good with the bad in many of his characters and sympathizes with them. In a way, as the nihilists have found, the resultant complexity of his work obscures his moral point and is detrimental to his rhetoric; but ultimately, as I hope to show in Chapter 5, it lends to his satire a subtlety and sophistication that makes it irresistibly persuasive.

Our discussion of the morality of satire in the *Ju-lin wai-shih* has thus far been general and abstract and it should be helpful to our understanding of Wu Ching-tzu's portrayal of the workings of *kung-ming fu-kuei* to consider a concrete example. Accordingly, let us examine the *Ju-lin wai-shih*'s account of the rise and fall of Kuang Chao-jen (Chapters 15–20), an unusual character in satirical literature inasmuch as he shows a clear and discernible degree of development, or rather, of degeneration.

IX   *Kuang Chao-jen as Fallen Hero*

The theme of conflict between virtue and learning and the desire for *kung-ming fu-kuei* is immediately indicated in Kuang Chao-jen's initial appearance. Ma Chun-shang finds him in a teashop diligently studying Ma's annotated compilation of examination essays and, on inquiry, discovers that he has just learned of his father's illness and is miserable because he lacks the funds to return to his distant home and fulfill his filial duties. "Tell me, friend," Ma asks him, "do you want to go on studying or to go back to see your father?" At the time, the question for Kuang is merely a practical one, with no implication of moral conflict. Therefore, he answers that he simply has no

money to carry on his studies, but would immediately prefer to see
his father since "as a son, if I cannot return to look after him, I
cannot even be compared to birds and beasts." Ma provides him
with the needed money and offers advice which amounts to a
justification of the principles of Confucian service to the state:

"Good brother, listen to me. When you return home, you should consider
passing the official examinations as the most important way of serving your
parents. There is no other way for men to achieve fame. . . . even teaching
and secretarial work are not proper careers. It is only if you have the
wherewithal to pass the examinations, to become a *chü-jen* or a *chin-shih*,
that you reflect credit upon your ancestors. That is what the *Book of Filial
Piety [Hsiao ching]* says: only to 'reflect credit on your family and to spread
personal fame' amount to the greatest filiality. At the same time, of course,
you do very well for yourself. As the ancient saying so nicely puts it, 'In
books there are golden mansions; in books there are thousands of bushels of
grain; in books there are women beautiful as jade.' And what can 'books' be
at present but our collections of examination essays? Good brother, when
you return to serve your parents, you must consider it of prime importance
to study for the examinations. . . . Writing essays is the main thing. For
when your father lies ill in bed with nothing to eat and hears you reciting
these essays, his heart will rejoice, and even though he clearly suffers, the
suffering will pass; even though he clearly is in pain, the pain will disappear.
This is what Tseng Tzu meant when he spoke of 'nurturing ambition.' For
even if you are not lucky enough to pass all the examinations, you should be
able to successfully compete for a position as a student on stipend and, later,
as an education official, you can also apply for titles for your parents. . . .[48]

Filial piety is what Nivison calls "the ultimate Confucian social
duty," and invoking it to justify taking the lesser course in the
intense conflict between the idealistic and the pragmatic or utilitarian is age-old, and is evident in the writings of Confucian
luminaries throughout Chinese history.[49] Men who entered public
service while realizing the obstacles this action presented to their
independent pursuit of learning and virtue would explain that the
material benefits it brought were necessary in order to be able to
provide for their parents' welfare. Ma goes even further, while ignoring the idealistic-pragmatic conflict and crudely equating high
Confucian virtue and duty with worldly fame, wealth, status, and
official titles. That the author completely disagrees can be seen in
the rest of the account of Kuang Chao-jen, an account which
amounts to a demonstration of the error of Ma's opinions.

Kuang's originally good character is graphically illustrated to the reader. From the moment Kuang reaches home, the author is careful to stress his filiality. He no sooner arrives than he goes about relieving his parents' material and spiritual anxieties. He greets his family with great humility and propriety and personally cooks a meal for his father, helping him to bed afterward and retiring himself at the foot of the bed to keep watch. The following day, he buys a few pigs and some beans and begins peddling pork and bean curd, keeping his earnings under his father's bed. He is not too busy to keep his father amused with lighthearted accounts of his travels. When his father indicates the need to defecate, Kuang refuses to allow him to go to the trouble of getting up, insisting that there is a better way.

Quickly he ran to the kitchen and brought out an earthenware pan, filling it with ashes and bringing it before the bed. Then he fetched a wooden bench and placed it on the other side of the pan. Crawling himself onto the bed, he helped his father over the gap, resting the latter's two feet on the bench and facing the latter's bottom squarely over the ashes in the pan. Kuang himself then crawled in between, kneeling on his knees and shouldering his father's two legs, allowing the old man to recline safely and steadily while comfortably completing his business. Then he straightened him out on the bed as before, thus easing the whole process and saving the bedding from stench. And after removing the bench and emptying the pan, Kuang came back in and sat down.[50]

To this point, Kuang Chao-jen is the picture of the dutiful son, resourceful and self-effacing in his filial piety. He is also shown to be frugal and industrious. Every day he gets up at the crack of dawn to sell his pork and bean curd and comes home by noon to keep his father company, not forgetting to buy special food to supplement the old man's diet. After his father retires, he studies late into the night. He also proves to be clever and diplomatic, time and again fending off the landlord-relative who is anxious to repossess their house. When a fire burns the house down, Kuang's one anxiety is the safety of his parents and sister-in-law, even as his brother scurries about to retrieve his own goods. The family moves to a new dwelling by a monastery, and Kuang continues his studies and his peddling, still tending to his father. If Kuang were to continue in this way, he would be no less exemplary than Wang Mien; but we soon see the difference. For while Wang Mien withdraws deter-

minedly from the enticements of officialdom, Kuang Chao-jen suc-
cumbs to them and both his character and his intellect begin a long
decline. This decline is first discernible toward the end of Chapter 16,
when Kuang meets the village magistrate Li Pen-ying who, having
overheard Kuang recite aloud to himself late at night, becomes
impressed and invites him, through the village headman, to take the
preliminary examinations. Unlike Wang Mien who literally flees
from the prospect of involvement with officialdom, Kuang eagerly
seizes this opportunity for advancement, passes the first examination, and becomes a favored pupil of the magistrate who rewards
him with money and personally intercedes on his behalf with the
imperial examiner. On the magistrate's recommendation, the
examiner agrees to pass Kuang in the prefectural examination for his
"high moral qualities" even though his essay lacks a certain amount
of clarity. Kuang thus sets foot in officialdom's door, and, at the start
of Chapter 17, we are shown, again without comment, the undesirable results.

First, we are told that Kuang's sick father, his son having gone to
the prefectural capital for the examinations, languishes in bed "with
his urine and his excrement," missing Kuang's ministrations so
much that "twenty days' absence seemed to him like two years."
Every day, with tears in his eyes, he frets over whether his son will
return in time to see him on his deathbed. Second, we find Kuang's
older brother quickly taking advantage of his sibling's newfound
status. In a fight with a fellow peddler in the marketplace, he is
ready to drag his adversary to court, shouting "The magistrate is a
friend of my brother's." Significantly, this bullying attitude further
disturbs his ailing father's peace of mind. Third, when the messen-
gers from the examination school arrive at the old man's house to
report his son's success, they become blatantly dissatisfied with the
tip of two hundred coins, even though that is all the money in the
house. Only after the old man's abject pleading and the intervention
of the village headman who personally adds to the tip are they
willing to leave. Finally, we are given the first glimpse of a flaw that
suddenly appears in Kuang's character—the arrogance and empty
pride which comes with worldly success. After being feted and honored by the villagers and by the magistrate "who now treated him as
an equal," Kuang is reluctant to pay the customary respects to the

more lowly country tutor, exclaiming that "I recognize only my own patron," and acquiescing only after the headman entreats him to do so. In this way, Kuang's success is shown to be have most undesirable results. Contrary to Ma Chun-shang's opinions, it clearly disturbs the peace and well-being of his dying father, thus demonstrating the inevitable conflict between the pursuit of fame and fortune and the fulfillment of filial duty. Just as significantly, it brings about Kuang's own moral decay. The subsequent death of his father removes the object of his exemplary filial piety and signals the downward turn of his character. The author, as he does elsewhere in the novel, uses the deathbed scene to reiterate his work's eremitic principles.[51] Kuang's father, in his final instructions, tells of the dangers of fame and fortune for personal development.

"Now my second son has been fortunate enough to pass the examinations. In the future, if he studies hard, he may even advance to a higher level. But fame is after all an external thing; it is virtuous conduct that is most important. You have concentrated on being a good son and a loyal brother, and that is very rare. I don't want you to see the world now in terms of wealth and power and change the character you had just because things will go relatively well for you in the future. After I'm gone and you've finished mourning, you must lose no time in finding a wife. But choose a girl from a poor family; don't try to better yourself by marrying into a family that is rich and noble. . . ."[52]

But Kuang is already too involved in striving for the fulfillment of his ambitions to be able to heed this advice, and his later involvement with the "wealth and power" his father warns him against leads to unfilial acts which mark the nadir of his moral decline.

Soon after the father's death, his patron the magistrate gets into trouble with his superiors, and Kuang again leaves his village for Hang-chou to escape possible repercussions. In the big city, Kuang becomes involved with a circle of pseudopoets, edits a volume of examination essays for a book dealer, and meets Pan Number Three who treats him like a brother and who involves him in a series of corrupt schemes. Later Pan arranges a marriage for Kuang with the daughter of a yamen runner, personally taking care of all expenses. Kuang's fortunes thus continue to improve, but we can see that his character suffers a corresponding decline. He learns that his patron

Magistrate Li has been vindicated and promoted to be a supervisory censor in the capital. At about the same time, he passes "first in the first rank" at the *sui* examination for *sheng-yüan* and is recommended to the Imperial College in the capital. Pan, meanwhile, gets arrested, but Kuang's only concern is for his own welfare as he hurries to the capital. This violation of *yi* or righteousness is quickly followed by the violation of *hsiao*, filial obedience. In the capital he lies about already having a wife because he is ashamed of her father's lowly occupation. Soon he finds himself unable to turn down his patron's offer to arrange a marriage with the latter's niece. In this way, his concern for status leads him to go directly against his father's final instructions.

But his situation continues to improve. He passes another examination and becomes an official tutor at the college, an achievement of sufficient import to require him to return to his own province for a testamonial from the local gentry. On reaching Hang-chou, Kuang finds that his first wife has died, largely from the unhappiness of being left alone with Kuang's family in the country. With no sense of guilt for having put her in that situation, Kuang's concern is to "make a portrait of her in her phoenix head-dress and embroidered costume" because "she is a lady now." He also becomes worried about his mother's rustic appearance, charging his brother to make her wear a nicer dress when she goes out so that she will "look different from the common herd." As for his brother, Kuang reminds him that, on returning to the village, "you must tell the villagers to address you as 'Sir,'" because "we'll have to live in style and keep up appearances" as the family is now of the official class.

This inordinate concern for appearances is enough to draw our disdain; but it is only the symptom of the real disease, his loss of the humane virtues. The subject of Pan's incarceration comes up again as Kuang is visited by a mutual friend and a yamen clerk who inform him that Pan is aware of his return and would like to see him to "talk over his troubles." Whereas a righteous man would not hesitate to come to the aid of anyone in need, and a benevolent man would sympathize with the misfortunes of a friend, Kuang is so puffed up by his new status that he not only refuses to help, but he justifies his refusal with preposterous pompousness. He tells his visitors that he is now "a servant of the throne" and thus must abide by the law. To visit Pan in prison "would show no respect for the law." When the clerk persists, arguing that "you can just consider it visiting a friend," Kuang becomes even more blunt: " 'In view of what Pan has done, if I had been in office here I would have had to arrest him. If I were to go to the prison to call on him, it would look as if I disapproved of the sentence. This is not the way of a loyal subject. . . . If I were to go to the jail and the story reached my superiors, my official reputation would be ruined. How can I do such a thing?' "⁵³ The reader of course will remember that, at the beginning of the chapter, when Kuang first learned of Pan's troubles, he was deeply worried because he had been involved in two of the cases listed in the arrest warrant.⁵⁴ It is this fact which makes the above statement so preposterous. Clearly, along with the loss of his filial piety, Kuang has also lost his benevolence and righteousness and become, in Confucian terms, a morally despicable man.

This moral collapse is accompanied by a corresponding stupidity, the sad destruction of a once promising intellect by the poison of ambition. We find Kuang Chao-jen bragging about the popularity of his publications, claiming that "scholars of the five northern provinces respect my name so highly that they often light incense and tapers to me on their desks, calling me 'Master Kuang of sacred memory.' " When it is pointed out to him that "Only the dead are described as 'of sacred memory,' " he is left with little to say.

The entire account of Kuang Chao-jen is presented in the manner of a scientific experiment, with a technique akin to modern naturalism. The author begins with a young man in a pristine state of moral virtue, injects the element of *kung-ming fu-kuei* and, without direct comment, allows the reader to witness the results. It is significant that Kuang Chao-jen is neither innately reprehensible nor the ultimate object of the satirist's censure. Kuang's only real fault, the only difference between him and Wang Mien, is his lack of the moral and intellectual awareness to resist the enticements of fame and fortune, to, in essence, remain content with the simple life so as to protect his moral and intellectual integrity.

X *Particular Themes*

Critics of the *Ju-lin wai-shih* have tended to dwell on its particular themes of social criticism: condemnation of the civil service examinations, of false propriety, of the unequal treatment of women, and of superstition.⁵⁵ It would be tedious and really unnecessary at this point to go into an exhaustive discussion of each of these themes. Suffice it to say that the satirist, in each case, attacks these social ills from the point of view of an idealistic Confucian, rigorously exposing the corruptive influence of the competitive quest for *kung-ming fu-kuei*. The examination system, the most visible part of this quest, is thus shown to be the most pervasively corruptive, monopolizing men's energies and turning them into moral and intellectual cripples. This is clear in the case of Kuang Chao-jen, as it is in the incident involving Chang Ching-chai and Fan Chin examined earlier, and we need not examine further examples.

In many parts of the *Ju-lin wai-shih*, as dunces struggle against each other for status and wealth, we find propriety, which in Confucian society governs the relationship of individuals in society, used as a shield for base motives, and what is the basis for a harmonious social order becoming the precise means of advancing hypocrisy and chaos. But whereas modern-day Chinese writers like Lu Hsün, who, in making the same analysis, advocate doing away with traditional propriety altogether, the satirist in the *Ju-lin wai-shih* advocates just the opposite. Firm in his Confucian faith, he sees the basic problem to arise not from propriety itself, but from society's corruption of it. Accordingly, the solution is seen to depend upon a return to true propriety, the symbolic representation of which is the highly ordered rituals to T'ai-po in Chapter 37. Confucius himself is supposed to have said that T'ai-po "attained to the very highest pitch of moral power" for his exemplification of the virtue of yielding, the very virtue all the dunces in the novel are shown to lack.[56] The account of the rituals themselves, as boring and mechanical as it may seem, is thus the central moral statement of the book, an expression of the hope that the revival of ancient rituals will also bring about the revival of humanistic values.[57] That the T'ai-po shrine falls into neglect (Chapter 48) and eventual ruin (Chapter 55) symbolizes what the satirist sees as the popular rejection of true propriety, not its invalidity.

Much has also been made of Wu Ching-tzu's role as spokesman for a kind of feminist equality.[58] Yet the few women who escape the author's satirical barbs in the *Ju-lin wai-shih*—most notably Chuang Shao-kuang's and Tu Shao-ching's (significantly) unnamed wives and Shen Chiung-chih (Shen Ch'iung-chih)—are presented with approval not so much because they are equal to men as because they are contented with their lot in life, or refuse to sacrifice personal integrity in the pursuit of status or wealth. In Chapter 34, Tu Shao-ching, in the course of interpreting a poem in the *Book of Poetry*, explicitly warns that wives too can be smitten by the desire for advancement and thus become quarrelsome, even though evidently his wife is not. For Tu the poem concerned is exemplary because it shows a couple who "play the lyre and drink" without the slightest desire for official rank.[59] Shen Chiung-chih, in turn, is praised for regarding the luxury and power she would have had as a salt merchant's concubine "like dirt and weeds," and for running off to live on her own terms by selling her poetry and art.[60] The primary values the author is advocating are thus clearly those of the eremitic, and are a far cry from twentieth-century feminism, either in China or in the West.

As for the *Ju-lin wai-shih*'s ideas on superstition, we should again beware about reading into them our own modernist concepts. For we can look long and hard and not find any clear-cut rejection of popular beliefs in the supernatural. Undeniably, the novel's approach to such matters is largely rational; yet what we would consider superstitious nonsense is far from absent. The strange wind and the appearance of a hundred and ten stars in Chapter 1 are given as omens to China's scholarly fortunes. Early on, we also encounter a dream and a Ouija-board fortune, both of which are shown to come true. Whatever Wu Ching-tzu's motives for including such accounts, we can see that his rejection of superstitious beliefs is not absolute. His oft-cited criticism of geomancy, therefore, should be seen not so much as a denial of superstition as an expression of revulsion for the lust for gain which superstition breeds. Geomancy, after all, is not really rejected in the *Ju-lin wai-shih*: even Dr. Yu the "true Confucian" is shown to be a practitioner, earning part of his livelihood by helping people select proper grave sites (Chapter 36). What bothers our satirist is the popular belief that a well-selected grave for one's parents can guarantee good fortune for the family. Proper geomancy is concerned only with fulfilling the filial duty of burying one's parents safely, in ground that is "dry and free from ants." But the people of Wu-ho (Chapters 44–45) are censured for wanting to prosper from their deceased parents, even delaying burials or exhuming and transferring remains to improve their own luck. To the author, this is tantamount to the heinous crime of parricide, and he proposes, through Tu Shao-ching, that those guilty ought to be executed "by being sliced into little pieces," so that this unnatural craze might be exterminated.[61]

We can now see that, indeed, there is a unified moral direction to the satire in the *Ju-lin wai-shih*. Positively, the novel espouses eremitic values, the cultivation of morality and intellect, the preservation of individual integrity. Negatively, it attacks the competitive quest for fame and wealth, for the *kung-ming fu-kuei* which directly and inevitably negate men's original goodness and talent. Many facts of Wu Ching-tzu's life—his father's lack of success in officialdom, his high regard for his father, his relative lack of success in the examinations, his alienation from the people of his hometown, his early decision to retire to Nanking, his identification with recluses in Chinese history—mesh perfectly with the moral concerns of his satire. In historical and biographical terms, the *Ju-lin wai-shih* may be seen as an elaborate apology for the author's personal choice of the life of withdrawal. Far from being distractions, these historical and biographical considerations are indispensible in helping us determine the meaning of a work obscured by time and social change. As we shall see in the following chapter, grasping this meaning is a precondition to achieving our primary goal, the recognition and evaluation of the skill of Wu Ching-tzu's craftsmanship and rhetoric— or we may say his art.

CHAPTER 4

Wit: Plot and Technique in the Ju-lin wai-shih

BECAUSE the previous chapter dwells almost exclusively on the morality of satire in the *Ju-lin wai-shih*, it may give the reader the notion that, in practice, this morality is distinct and separate from the wit which formulates it and gives it existence.[1] This would be a grievous mistake. Good satire is a natural unity of morality and wit: the need to convey a given truth determines and takes on a form proper to itself. It is for this reason that the study of satirical wit must begin with an understanding of satirical morality.

As wit in satire is interwoven with the moral need to persuade and teach, it is basically rhetorical and should be examined with this fact in mind. If satirical narrative, like other narrative forms, does imitate reality, it does so not for "aesthetic" reasons, or because of an author's desire to create a "world." Rather, it aims to reach out to its readers, via the bridge of common perceptions of reality, in order to lead them to accept its moral tenets. Whether it does this well or poorly should be the primary concern of those who would assess its ultimate worth. In discussing the plot and technique of the *Ju-lin wai-shih*, however, no one, including the Marxists, has bothered to consider them as functions of the work's moral concern. Instead, we find a common tendency to label the *Ju-lin wai-shih* a work of "realism," either in the Marxist or the eighteenth-century European sense, with little consideration of its essentially rhetorical character. The result is a continuing confusion and much irrelevant criticism.

A critic of realistic fiction, for example, has a natural tendency to look for a close-knit plot, to seek out, as Kernan puts it, "a tightly constructed chain of cause and effect moving inevitably towards a conclusion," forming a self-contained and self-explanatory world.[2] The technical features he expects to analyze—diction, tone, point of view, characterization, and so forth—should ideally evolve from and support this world, producing what C. T. Hsia has called "a unified impression of life as conceived and planned by a master intelligence."[3] Most works of satire, including Western satire, would fail to meet these specifications for the simple reason that satire is created for a different purpose and evinces a different concern. As we shall see, the *Ju-lin wai-shih* is put together with a tantalizing amount of realistic portrayals; but judging it in terms of realism alone can blind a critic to its artistic features. In considering the *Ju-lin wai-shih*'s plot and technique, therefore, we should keep foremost in our minds its essentially rhetorical and didactic nature. For whatever wit it displays can most accurately be discovered and evaluated as a consequence of its drive to teach and persuade.

I *Plot in the* Ju-lin wai-shih

That the *Ju-lin wai-shih* lacks an all-encompassing plot is a common judgment of critics from dynastic times to the present. In the opinion of one early anonymous commentator, the author "did not decide in the beginning the number of characters or episodes to include before stopping" and, as a result, the book "can be concluded any place, or cannot be concluded any place."[4] Hu Shih, writing in the early 1920s, concluded that the *Ju-lin wai-shih* has no real plot, that it consists "completely of short stories linked together one by one. Split them up, and each becomes a whole; string them together, and they become endless."[5] In more recent times, we find a similar opinion expressed by Liu Wu-chi, who writes that the *Ju-lin wai-shih* "suffers from a basic weakness . . . the lack of organic structure," and that "The links between the episodes are so weak and ineffectual that the book might as well be divided into a number of separate stories."[6]

In each of these cases, it is clear that the critic comes to the *Ju-lin wai-shih* with artistic expectations derived from nonsatirical fiction. Kernan has pointed out that, in the West as well, satire's need to "illustrate and drive home a thesis" causes it to take on a plot structure which appears to be "a succession of seemingly loosely related events with little apparent development." Readers may expect the "direct, linear progression which is ordinarily taken as plot"; but in satire, they only get "collections of loosely related scenes and business which curls back on itself" and "darkness" which "never really moves on to daylight but only to intensified darkness."[7] Cultural differences aside, the plot of the *Ju-lin wai-shih* fits this description well. For Wu Ching-tzu, like his Western counterparts, evidently

finds the macroscopic presentation of scene upon scene and character upon character more suited to his didactic purposes than the
microscopic exploration we have come to expect in fiction of a more
expressive or objective orientation. To say that the *Ju-lin wai-shih* is
plotless is therefore to accept only a narrow definition of plot. It
would be preferable to follow Kernan's advice and consider as plot
any *action* or *movement* in a work of literature. This would allow us
"to take our plots where and how we find them" rather than to
prescribe a priori theories and rules. [8]

And at any rate, it is important to see that while cause and effect
are not firmly established from one episode to another in the *Ju-lin
wai-shih*, the work as a whole does show a definite design. We have
seen in the previous chapter that the author sandwiches his satire
between two morality tales of exemplary models, and present a
symbolic affirmation of this same morality about two-thirds of the
way through. This design is what enables the reader to constantly
check his moral compass and grasp the ironical character of the plot.

Even more than humor, irony is an almost inseparable companion
of satire. In essence, irony is that which presents a situation, spoken
or dramatized, in which "what seems to be and what is are in some
way opposed." [9] Kernan, who gives this definition, goes on to explain that, in the Western satires he studies, the dark energies
which trace out the satirical plot almost invariably seek to "drive a
wedge between appearance and reality." Moreover, while irony in
other kinds of literature can blend into ambiguity, tension, paradox,
or ambivalence, what is and what seems to be are usually kept
separate in satire in order to fulfill the didactic purpose. Dunces can
be seen to magnify themselves, but the magnification itself becomes
a dimunition; they seek to rise, but their ascent becomes an actual
decline; they drive forward toward a certain order, but the order
invariably becomes chaos.

It is easy to see that this description applies also to the action or
movement (that is, plot) of the *Ju-lin wai-shih* where, after the
establishment of the moral standards, example after example is
given of dunces who, enticed by *kung-ming fu-kuei*, unknowingly
and uncontrollably violate these standards in a multitude of ways
while ironically defeating themselves. Kuang Chao-jen's self-mag-
nifying speech—that as a tutor in the Imperial College, he uses a
kingly "vermillion brush" to mark his students' papers, that even his
lowest-ranking charges will become "provincial governors or gener-

als," that his own teacher is the son of the prime minister, etc.—is precisely what diminishes him in our estimation.[10] Fan Chin and Hsun Mei (Hsün Mei) finally achieve the official status they have been seeking for years; but, in each case, their hard-earned success amounts to a moral fall. Fan is shown to use his mother's death to his own advantage, pressuring another official into contributing to the funeral, when a properly filial son would be solely concerned with proper mourning. His ultimate hypocrisy is cleverly illustrated at the banquet he subsequently attends where, as one still in mourning, he insists on using unadorned utensils instead of the silver-inlaid ones set before him. As the narrator relates it, the host remains anxious until he spies Fan popping "a large shrimp ball from the dish of bird's-nests into his mouth."[11] Hsun Mei, whose mother also passes away just as he achieves examination success, proves easily persuadable to withhold the news from his superiors because the period of mourning he would otherwise have to observe would hinder his chances of obtaining a good appointment.[12]

The cumulative effect of such accounts of moral misdirection is the inescapable impression of a topsy-turvy world, a world of hypocrites and fools who strive for outer appearances rather than for inner substance and who inevitably defeat themselves. We find Niu Pu-lang (Niu P'u-lang) masquerading as the poet Niu Pu-yi, thus substituting a famous name for actual learning; and we watch with a mixture of disgust and amusement as he fights with his brothers-in-law and becomes involved with a shady member of the gentry at whose hands he is eventually bound, stripped, beaten, and thrown by the side of a cesspool.[13] In a more widely quoted account, we see that Chou Chin, forced to give up the examination life in which, for almost a lifetime, he was bullied and insulted for his repeated failures, is too dull to recognize the cause of his problems, and wails from cell to cell in an examination school he visits, ultimately knocking himself out against a desk.[14] Multiply these examples for the length of the novel and we have a composite picture of a discordant society in almost hopeless chaos. As the narrator sums up in the beginning of Chapter 55:

Pleasure haunts and taverns were no longer frequented by men of talent, and worthy men no longer occupied themselves with ceremony and letters. As for scholarship, all who passed the examinations were considered brilliant, and all who failed fools. As for liberality, the rich indulged in ostentatious gestures while the poor were forced to seem shabby. You might have the genius of a Li Po or a Tu Fu, or the moral worth of a Yen Hui or a Tseng Shen, but no one would come to ask your advice. So at coming of age ceremonies, marriages, funerals, or sacrifices in big families and in the halls of the local gentry, nothing was discussed but promotions, transfers, and recalls in the official world. And all the impecunious scholars did was to try by various tricks to find favor with the examiners. . . .[15]

The plot design of the *Ju-lin wai-shih*, which juxtaposes paragons and dunces and virtue and vice, comes clearly from the intention of the satirist to convey this picture. The opening account of Wang Mien allows us to understand the irony ruling the action of all the dunces; the closing account of the four eccentrics makes us reflect back and understand subtleties we might have missed. The positing of this gap between worldly status and actual worth, between examination success and real learning, and between the attainment of wealth and the attainment of virtue is what makes irony a structural feature of the plot and what gives it a kind of unity despite its seeming lack of connectives between episodes. As rhetoric, this ironic structure achieves its effect by placing the reader on a higher plane of knowledge, allowing him to observe the consequences of moral confusion not apparent to the dunces themselves.

II *Structural Unevenness*

Even in these terms, however, the plot of the *Ju-lin wai-shih* (as we have it today) fails to reveal a finished unity, and I do not want to leave the impression that it does. The likely causes are both external and internal. Externally, as in many traditional Chinese novels, there is the nagging possibility of later interpolation or indiscriminate revision, possibilities not to be ignored even though they still cannot be proved.[16] Parts of three to four chapters immediately following the one on the T'ai-po rituals (Chapter 37) are rather poorly written, in terms of both style and content, with careless contradictions and easy excursions into fantasy not to be found in the rest of the novel.[17] These lapses, of course, may be Wu Ching-tzu's own, perhaps hasty jottings intended for later revision. In the absence of proof, we can do no more than to note them.

When we consider internal causes for the novel's unevenness, we have more solid ground for speculation. Ho Tse-han's work has shown us that Wu Ching-tzu incorporated popular vignettes, jokes,

and stories freely into the *Ju-lin wai-shih*, and we have seen that
some of them do not mesh smoothly with the work's basic satirical
intent.[18] Moreover, as mentioned previously, there are indications
that Wu Ching-tzu tried to pattern his plot in some fashion after the
plot of the *Water Margin*, with mixed results.[19] The account of one
hundred and ten little stars falling to the southeast and Wang Mien's
linking of this to the belated maintenance of China's scholarly fortunes does not seem at all relevant to the satirical import of the
book. This incident can best be understood as a rather feeble attempt to follow the *Water Margin*'s opening tale of Commander
Hung (Hung T'ai-wei) who, in Pandora fashion, raises a long buried
stone slab, thus releasing a black cloud of demons which shoots up
to the sky where it is transformed "into a hundred-odd shafts of
golden light" scattering in all directions. Later, it becomes obvious
that each shaft of light represents one of the hundred and eight
bandit heroes who eventually gather at the famous lair in Liang-
shan.[20] To the end of Chapter 70 in its hundred and twenty chapters, the *Water Margin* is taken up with rambling accounts of the
odysseys of its many heroes from citizen to outlaw. In the *Ju-lin
wai-shih*, this format of character following character and episode
following episode, with rather weak linkages in between, works well
for satire, allowing the narrator to scan all levels of society and to
display fully the chaos-making tendencies of dunces of all sorts
scampering after *kung-ming fu-kuei*. The eventual gathering at
T'ai-po and the rituals performed there correspond well to the
climactic gathering of the robber band at Liang-shan and to the
ceremonies of brotherhood and the expressions of gratitude to
heaven and earth which the robbers carry out as a kind of moralistic
statement and justification. Thereafter, the band proceeds to engage
in various military campaigns, some on behalf of the government to
which they surrender, before perishing at the hands of villains. This
later part of the plot format is what proves far less suited to the *Ju-lin
wai-shih*'s satiric needs.

It appears that immediately following the T'ai-po account, the
author again loses his satirical perspective and wanders into the area
of exemplary fiction with the confused and sometimes naive account
of Kuo Li, the "filial son" who undergoes a series of wild adventures
on his journey in search of a lost father. Kuo is first introduced as an
old man "haggard and thin" with graying hair and beard.[21] Soon
after, however, a robber is said to become frightened of Kuo be-

cause he appears to be "hefty and strong."[22] On his travels, Kuo indeed alternates between being strong and weak. Sometimes he displays enough martial skill to remind us of the *Water Margin* hero Lin Ch'ung, converting would-be assailants to willing disciples; at other times he is as weak and helpless as Tripitaka in *Journey to the West (Hsi-yu chi)*. Once, in an incident combining elements from both of these novels, Kuo meets up with a tiger in a forest. But instead of devouring him, this tiger places him in a pit and goes off, returning subsequently with a fantastic white beast with a single horn and "eyes like huge red lanterns." Meanwhile, Kuo has found refuge in a tree and watches as this unicorn first dispatches the tiger in anger and then impales himself on a branch while lunging at Kuo. This account, along with those dealing with the military exploits of Hsiao Yun-hsien (Hsiao Yün-hsien) and Brigade General Tang (T'ang), is clearly out of character with the rest of the novel. When Hsiao's and Tang's respective successes are shown to be rewarded only with demotion, fines, and reprimands, however, we can feel the plot resuming its satirical direction. And except for yet another diversion in the comic account of the knight-errant Feng Ming-chi (Feng Ming-ch'i) in Chapters 50–52, satire remains the principal direction to the very end.[23]

As long as the possibility of interpolation and/or revision exists, it is impossible to say to what extent Wu Ching-tzu is responsible for these lapses in his plot. We can only conclude that, as we have it, the plot of the *Ju-lin wai-shih* could have benifitted from careful editing. On the other hand, its overall design and general movement can be said to present a moral vision with a goodly amount of irony and indirection, and we can validly call it satirical.

This label affirms its fundamental similarity with all satirical literature, whether in China or in the West. This study, however, is more concerned with the *Ju-lin wai-shih*'s unique qualities, with its particular brand of satire. We should, therefore, proceed to a consideration of its satirical technique, of the particular ways it presents its moral criticism. These ways can best be understood and appreciated in the company of those employed by the traditional Chinese storyteller and the traditional Chinese historian or man of letters.

III *The Technique of the Historian*

The greater part of the Chinese literary tradition is certainly pragmatic: that is, its foremost concern is the effect on the reader. In discussing the *Ju-lin wai-shih*, it is helpful to divide this pragmatic aim into two: the didactic and the entertaining. Under the continuing influence of Confucianism, orthodox literature (which includes history) was charged with the serious mission of instructing the reader and thereby bettering society. In popular writings such as fiction, however, entertainment becomes the paramount value, even though ample lip service continued to be paid to high morality. As didactic literature in popular dress, the *Ju-lin wai-shih* straddles both categories, and we should expect to find in it a technique combining the influences of both the classical litterateur and the teller of popular tales.

A deeply committed moralist who infuses his writing with Confucian concerns, Wu Ching-tzu calls his novel an "unofficial history." It is unofficial because it is consciously fictionalized and couched in the vernacular language for easier comprehension and enjoyment; but it is history because it nevertheless presents serious moral truths in the manner of a traditional historian. In considering the technique of satire in the *Ju-lin wai-shih*, the critic cannot therefore afford to ignore either end of this unique and interesting combination, a combination which accounts for both the strengths and the weaknesses of the novel's satirical art.

Credit for pointing out the influence of Chinese historical writings on the drafting of the *Ju-lin wai-shih* must be accorded to the Chinese Marxist critic Wu Tsu-hsiang who characterized its narrative method as *shih-pi*, or "historiographical technique." Traditional Chinese historians, as Wu explains, were influenced by the practice, attributed to Confucius himself, of couching moral approval or censure (*yü pao-pien*) in the selective but noncommittal presentation of facts, and thus practiced *p'i-li yang-ch'iu*, or "[subtly and indirectly] indicating critical judgment beneath a noncommittal surface."[24] There is no question but that this elliptical, concentrated, and suggestive narrative method, heretofore the province of classical historiography, is prominent in the *Ju-lin wai-shih*. Like the reader of the official histories, the reader of the *Ju-lin wai-shih* is constantly called upon to look beneath the objective pose for the subjectivity within and to be alert for seemingly insignificant facts which may carry deep meanings. In our earlier discussion of Chang Ching-chai and Fan Chin visiting the magistrate of Kaoyao, we saw this technique at work: the narrator never tells the reader that

Chang and Fan are fuzzy-minded pedants; it is the reader who comes to this conclusion after examining the surface particulars.

As a further illustration, we can consider the initial appearance of the hapless scholar Chou Chin on the occasion of his arrival at Hsüeh Market where a welcoming banquet awaits him as the new village schoolmaster.

On the sixteenth the villagers sent in contributions to Shen Hsiang-fu who prepared a feast for the new teacher, a feast to which he also invited Mei Chiu, the new scholar in the village. Mei Chiu arrived early, wearing his new square cap, but Chou Chin did not turn up till nearly noon. When dogs started barking outside, Shen Hsiang-fu went out to welcome the guest; and the villagers stared as Chou came in. He was wearing an old felt cap, a tattered gray silk gown, the right sleeve and seat of which were in shreds, and a pair of shabby red silk slippers. He had a thin, dark face, and a beard flecked with white. Shen escorted him in, and only then did Mei Chiu rise slowly to greet him.

"Who is this gentleman?" asked Chou.

They told him, "He is Mr. Mei, our village scholar."

When Chou Chin heard this, he declared it would be presumptious to allow Mei to bow to him. "Today is different," Mei said, but Chou steadfastly refused.

"You are older than he is," said the villagers. "So please let things be as they should."

But Mei Chiu rounded on them, "You people don't understand the rule of our school. Those who have passed the prefectural examination are considered senior to those who have not, regardless of age. But today happens to be exceptional, and Mr. Chou must still be honored."[25]

The hasty reader can easily be taken in by the passionless, even tone of this passage and miss the satirical barbs hidden everywhere beneath the surface calm. It is important to notice from the start that the inclusion of the new scholar Mei Chiu in the banquet sets up yet another round in the unending competition for status. Armed with his new degree, as signified by his scholar's cap, Mei Chiu is eager and arrives early to assert his superiority over the supposed guest of honor, whose lateness indicates apprehensions and timidity. Indeed, the suggestion is that Chou is in such a sorry state even dogs tend to bark at him. When he appears, we are given the reason for his lack of confidence: his "old felt cap" shows that he has never earned the badge of status which belongs to his would-be adversary, even though the worn-out places in his garment indicate the many hours he must have spent leaning on his right elbow as he rereads his books and rewrites his compositions. In terms of social position, Chou is no match for Mei, but, in the brief description of the former's features, we are reminded of the moral respect he rightfully should command as a man of greater age and seniority. The rest of the account turns on the ignoring of this consideration in the face of the pride of status brought on by even a lowly examination degree. We see that neither Mei, the offender, nor Chou, the victim, are at all aware of any impropriety in the former's hesitant greeting. Indeed, Chou is so convinced of his own inferiority that he refuses to accept a simple bow; and Mei is really agreeing with Chou when he protests, not once but twice, that the occasion calls for the suspension of ordinary rules of decorum, meaning that, in the usual case, he is of too high a status to accord Chou even a slight show of deference. Ironically, it is the unlettered bystanders who show that they know better by insisting on Chou's rights.

Typically, the satirist does not bother to specify these points, as if they are clear and obvious. He relies on the reader's own moral sense to become angered and to lead him naturally to the satirist's point of view. The advantages of such a rhetorical technique remains to be enumerated; but we can see the demands it places on the reader. In the *Ju-lin wai-shih*, just as Chinese fiction takes on a dominant moral seriousness in place of its usually comical or romantic bent, its technical features have also changed from the narrator's subjective intrusion to the objective pose, from denotative exhaustiveness to connotative suggestion, from blatant assertion to subtle indirection. Such features belong to the classical mode, a mode which stresses subtlety and sophistication in contrast to the overstatements and the sensationalism found in most earlier fiction, which catered more to the need for recreation and fun.[26] The argument can therefore be made that the *Ju-lin wai-shih* is essentially classical in nature.

IV *The Technique of the Storyteller*

And yet the *Ju-lin wai-shih* also has its undeniable affinity to popular literature. To discount this affinity would be to ignore its many other significant features—features attributable to the tradition of the teller of popular tales. Most obviously, Wu Ching-tzu chose to render his novel in a nonliterary language, and thus to place it also into the tradition of vernacular Chinese fiction, a tradition which never completely shed the trappings of storytellers who entertained semiliterate and illiterate audiences in the temple yards and the marketplaces of China since at least the T'ang dynasty.[27] We find, therefore, that Wu Ching-tzu divides his work into *hui* or "sessions" (which I have called "chapters"), each headed by an antithetical couplet and begun with the phrase-marker "*hua-shuo*" or "The story goes that . . . ," followed by a brief summary of what has occurred immediately before. Each *hui*, moreover, ends with a hint of what is to follow, using such stock storyteller phrases as "*wei-chih . . . ju-ho*" ("We don't know what's to transpire next") and "*ch'ieh t'ing hsia-hui fen-chieh*" ("Let's listen to the explanation in the next session").

But the influence of the storyteller tradition of course goes far deeper than the superficial and the formulaic. To see how this influence blends—sometimes smoothly, sometimes not—with the classical character of the *Ju-lin wai-shih*, we can conveniently refer to the three modes by which P. D. Hanan, in his study of Chinese vernacular fiction of the sixteenth century, distinguishes vernacular narrative from its classical counterpart.[28] These modes are listed as "description," "presentation," and "commentary," and we can, in terms of each mode, see how Wu Ching-tzu's narrative technique is linked to that of the popular raconteur as well.

At first glance, it would appear that the *Ju-lin wai-shih*'s mode of description owes nothing to previous vernacular fiction. Nowhere in it do we find the traditional stereotyped verses in parallel prose and what Hanan calls "rather overblown imagery." Its descriptions, such as that for Chou Chin in the passage above, blend completely into the rest of the narrative, and the traditional phrase markers which were used to introduce the mode are discarded altogether. Chou Chin is said to have a thin, dark face and a whitish beard; he wears an old felt cap and a gown tattered in certain places—each point individualized and, more important, each point adding to the impression that Chou is a poor, frustrated scholar. In the *Ju-lin wai-shih*, what is a distracting and extraneous remnant from the oral storyteller tradition becomes an integral part of the written narrative.

Undeniably, this advancement in literary craftsmanship is due largely to classical influences. Yet, despite its concurrent suggestiveness, the particularity of detail and the sharpness of characterization in the description of Chou Chin indicate that the explicitness characteristic of vernacular fiction is not altogether absent, and that the mode of description in the *Ju-lin wai shih* can more accurately be seen as a blend of both classical and vernacular narrative techniques. This combination—of suggestiveness on the one hand and explicitness on the other—is also evident in Wu Ching-tzu's descriptions of scenery. The passage in Chapter 1 detailing the lovely freshness of a lake and its surroundings after a sudden shower is usually cited as an example of Wu's contribution to the full development of the descriptive mode in vernacular Chinese fiction. But even more impressive is his later account of the urban bustle of his beloved Nanking:

After the middle of the fourth month in Nanking, the Ch'in-huai river becomes quite lovely. Then barges from other tributaries of the Yangtze dismantle their cabins, set up awnings, and paddle into the river. Each vessel carries a small, square, gilt-lacquered table, set with an Yi-hsing stoneware pot, cups of the finest Cheng-hua or Hsüan-te porcelain, and the choicest tea brewed with rain water. Boating parties bring wine, hors d'oeuvres, and sweetmeats with them to the canal, and even people travelling by boat order a few cents' worth of good tea to drink on board as they proceed slowly on their way. At dusk two bright horn lanterns on each vessel are reflected in the water as the barges ply to and fro, so that both above and below are bright. Fluting and singing are heard all night and every night from Literary Virtue Bridge to Lucky Crossing Bridge and East Water Gate. The pleasure-goers buy water-rat fireworks too, which project from the water and look like pear trees in blossom when let off. The fun goes on till the fourth watch each night.[29]

Rendered in fluent vernacular Chinese, such descriptions are a new technical feature of popular Chinese fiction of the eighteenth century.

With respect to the mode of presentation, which "consists of dialogue and narrated action, and makes up the greater part of the work," Hanan points out that older vernacular fiction is rendered from the point of view of a blunt and obtrusive narrator "who assumes the persona of a public story-teller addressing his audience." By adopting the formulaic trappings of this tradition, Wu Ching-tzu also assumes this narrative position and, at least sometimes, talks down to his readers. At the same time, Wu's narrator is more hidden and more indirect, often assuming, as we have seen, an objective pose, wielding his barbs from behind a noncommittal exterior, and allowing the reader to make up his own mind. The result of this mixture of techniques is a tempering of the elliptical terseness, which is so much a part of the objective pose, with paradoxical exhaustiveness which allows for sharp delineations of character and an occasional show of exuberance. Consider the reaction of Fan Chin's father-in-law Butcher Hu (Hu T'u-hu) when Fan comes to him for money to finance his journey to the provincial capital to take the *chü-jen* examination:

Butcher Hu spat in his face and poured out a torrent of abuse. "Don't forget who you are!" he roared. "You're a toad, and just because you've got a bit of success, you go off thinking you can taste the flesh of heavenly swans! And I hear that you scraped through not because of your essay, but because the examiner pitied you for being so old. Now, like a fool, you want to be a provincial graduate! People who pass at that level are all stars in heaven! Don't you see those officials from the Chang family in town? They have piles of money, and each one has a dignified face and large ears. With that sharp little mouth and those monkey cheeks of yours, you should piss on the ground and take a look at your own reflection. You don't even know what's going on, and you want to hang around high-class behinds! . . ." He went on with one thing after another, until Fan's head spun.[30]

Such highly individualized and lively speeches would be absent if Wu Ching-tzu adhered only to the classical spirit he introduces to vernacular fiction.

V Mode of Commentary

While commentary is also common to historical narrative, it is clear that, in the *Ju-lin wai-shih*, this mode is expressed in a manner derived from the vernacular storyteller. Hanan explains that, in older vernacular fiction, the mode of commentary usually includes "introductory remarks or prologue, explanations given during the course of the narrative, comments both in verse and prose, and the summaries." That the *Ju-lin wai-shih* adopts this particular mode is evident from the very outset, when the narrator expresses his regret that men will always risk their lives "in search of riches, rank, success, and fame." And while this type of explicit intrusion must maintain a sometimes uneasy partnership with the more detached classical manner, direct remarks and explanations from the narrator are found throughout the novel. Except for Chapters 1 and 55, each chapter closes with an explicit commentary in a poetic couplet, clearly marked off by a phrase, such as *yu-fen-chiao* ("It will come about that . . ."), and each verse indicating what is to occur immediately thereafter.

One example of this feature should suffice. At the end of Chapter 2, after Chou Chin's tragicomical display in the examination cell, the narrator comes forward to tell us that "After years of frustration, he will unexpectedly meet up with wind and clouds [that is, attain a high position],/ In the pitiful state of his declining years, he will actually be able to see the lofty moon and sun."[31] Such commentary is, of course, formulaic and completely within the tradition of Chinese vernacular fiction. Its presence throughout the *Ju-lin wai-shih* has the age-old effects of distancing the narrator from the action of the story itself and of repeatedly reasserting his omniscience.

Intrusive commentary is moreover not limited to the formulaic; it also appears with little warning in the middle of otherwise objectively presented passages. Immediately following the objectively reported exchange between Mei Chiu and Chou Chin quoted above, the narrator abruptly enters the scene to restate the point with a rather unnecessary aside:

Actually Ming dynasty scholars called all those who passed the prefectural examinations "classmates," and those who only qualified for this examination "juniors." A young man in his teens who passed was considered senior to an unsuccessful candidate, even if the latter were eighty years old. It was like the case of a concubine. A woman is called "new wife" when she marries, and later "mistress"; but a concubine remains "new wife" even when her hair is white.[32]

Or, with the introduction of the Lou brothers (Chapter 8), the narrator jumps back in time to provide the reader with appropriate background information, marking his commentary with the phrase-marker *na-chih:* "The fact was that [*na-chih*] because these two brothers had failed in the metropolitan examination and were unable to enter the Han-lin Academy, they held a perpetual grudge against society. They were always declaring that since the Yung-lo Emperor usurped the throne, the Ming dynasty has gone to the dogs."[33]

In this latter case, the intrusion provides information necessary for the full understanding of the account, while in much of the novel, facts and conversations are so presented that the satirical point is made without any commentary at all. Still, it is undeniable that the mode of commentary borrowed from traditional vernacular fiction is also a prominent feature of the narrative style of the *Ju-lin wai-shih*, the satirical art of which is affected by this borrowing.

It is true that, as a whole, the *Ju-lin wai-shih* still differs greatly from the storyteller fiction it partially imitates. The invariably clear markings of transition from one mode to another which Hanan finds in early fiction are not always so clear in the hybrid narrative of the *Ju-lin wai-shih*. In fact, in its most polished parts, as in much of the account of Kuang Chao-jen, we find the merging together of description, presentation, and commentary until they are one and inseparable: a character is really described by what he says and does, and his words and actions in turn make a clear, if unspoken, moral comment. Nevertheless, it is also true that the role assumed by the narrator—the most crucial determinant of narrative art—is mostly limited by the novel's adherence to the mode of commentary of the vernacular storyteller.

VI *The Importance of the Narrator*

In most later Western satirical works, artistic distance is maintained between the actual author and his narrator-persona. R. C. Elliott has shown that these narrators, even as they castigate the faults and foibles of their satirical objects, are themselves tainted and culpable.[34] This distancing or "removal of the author by one step at least from his satire" converts the narrator from a *personal* attacking voice to a *dramatic* figure with a direct role in the narrative or play, thus doubling the possibility of irony and bringing into play the full range of satirical techniques. In the *Ju-lin wai-shih*, however, the distance exists not between the author and narrator, but, owing to the mode of commentary, actually between the narrator and the rest of the characters. Far from becoming a dramatic participant in the action, this narrator remains either invisible or, when he does appear, he steps forward to provide summaries, information, or comment, but always from a detached and omniscient vantage point. Moreover, while the technique of what Elliott calls "the satirist satirized" in Western literature indicates the authors' recognition of "their own involvement in the folly of human life," the narrator of the *Ju-lin wai-shih*, as the author's direct voice, is never questioned concerning either the rightness of his morality or the

folly or evil in the dunces he presents. One result is a certain limita-
tion of the range of satirical techniques, since what Kernan, following Pope, calls "dullness" can be shown to operate only among the
characters themselves.

Nowhere in the *Ju-lin wai-shih* do we find satirical allegory or
metaphor, not even in dream sequences; the narrator seems to be
too serious and straightforward to delve into such things.[35] Neither
do we encounter the double irony associated with a dramatically
involved narrator who, like Swift's modest proposer, is himself a
dunce. Nor is there parody or burlesque, as is usually found in a
narrator with a more playful and less moralistic attitude. The direct
commentary we do encounter is generally free of irony and satirical
intent, with some exceptions in the Wu-ho chapters which, in any
case, lean more toward invective than genuine satire. In searching
for satire in the *Ju-lin wai-shih*, therefore, we should shift our focus
from the narrator, who seldom deviates from the onmiscient, serious role of a direct recorder of events, to the characters who together act out the drama of dullness.

We should keep in mind, on the other hand, that this role is
indeed only a pose. Just as a newsreel camera scans the landscape to
record only what it wishes, the narrator in the *Ju-lin wai-shih* is
constantly picking out for the reader's perusal only those things
which have a bearing on his satirical intent. The parts of the novel
quoted throughout this study should make this obvious. The reader
is constantly made to observe certain facts (such as Chou Chin's
appearance) or actions (Fan Chin eating his shrimp) which contrib-
ute to the moral point; and he is allowed to overhear certain conversations (like that of the picnickers Wang Mien encounters) which
demonstrate the workings of dullness.

VII   *The Art of Wu Ching-tzu*

It is in the recording of such conversations, in fact, that Wu
Ching-tzu's art is at its subtle best. For this reason, it would not be
excessive for us to examine another example. Chapter 23 contains
the scene of Niu Pu-lang talking to a Taoist priest, a conversation in
which Niu, recently rebuffed and neglected by his travel companion, tries to bolster his own ego:

"I used to be in Magistrate Tung's yamen in Antung County. He's really a
hospitable gentleman. I remember when I first went there; I no sooner

presented my card than he sent two attendants out to meet my palanquin. I wasn't in a palanquin however, but was riding on a donkey; and when I wanted to alight, the attendants wouldn't let me. The two of them led my donkey straight into the pavillion, the donkey's hooves going clopety-clop on the wooden floor. Magistrate Tung had already opened his gate and came forward himself to greet me, and we entered hand in hand. He kept me there for over twenty days. When I wanted to leave, he presented me with seventeen taels and forty-five cents of fine silver, escorting me to the hall and seeing me on my donkey. 'If you do well elsewhere, so much the better,' he said. 'If not, come back to me again.' There are not many men like that! I am on my way back to him now."[36]

From what has already been related, the reader knows that this is an elaborate fabrication: Niu has never been to Magistrate Tung's yamen in Antung. But this fabrication is not pure fantasy; instead, it is interlaced, as in so many lies, with bits of truth. Niu is actually acquainted with the magistrate who, mistaking him for the poet Niu Pu-yi, had once visited him (Chapter 22). Moreover, Tung had recently become the magistrate of Antung and did, on the occasion of his visit, invite Niu to see him in his yamen. By "objectively" reproducing Niu's speech, the satirist is allowing the reader to pick out and note the fabricated parts and, in the process, deepening the reader's acquaintance with the workings of dullness in this one particular mind.

It is clear, for example, that Niu is blessed with a crafty imagination: he fabricates with great realism and detail, fancying himself a wandering scholar on a donkey who is eagerly welcomed as a man of learning by persons of high status. He does not forget that his imaginary donkey would make noises with its hooves as it walks on the wooden floors of an official's residence, that the magistrate would show his regard by taking his hand, even though he goes somewhat overboard in mentioning the unlikely detail of the forty-five cents change in the parting monetary gift. A closer reading would reveal the thoroughly believable workings of an inventive mind intent on providing the impression of an imaginary high status. Niu first mentions that he arrives in a palanquin, but quickly realizes the implausibility of that claim since only persons of great wealth ever go about in that manner. So he cleverly shifts his mistake over to Magistrate Tung who, supposedly thinking that Niu would be in a palanquin, sends his attendants out to greet him. Niu also does not forget to add that the attendants do not allow him to walk, but lead his donkey, as if it were a palanquin, straight into the magistrate's inner quarters. Of the imaginary departure, Niu does not merely say that the magistrate gives him silver, but "seventeen taels and forty-five cents of *fine* silver." And, in adding Tung's supposed parting instructions, Niu is implying that he knows other men of status who would receive him in the same deferential manner.[37] It is this yearning for social importance, now thoroughly impressed on the reader, that motivates Niu; that twists the directions of his not unintelligent mind toward empty fabrications rather than toward learning and truth; that, in short, makes him a dunce.

VIII   *Effects of Wu Ching-tzu's Satire*

Wu Ching-tzu's narrator may now and then intrude to comment on the action, but he stops short of making ultimate judgments for the reader. More like the Confucian historian, he prefers to present facts or record conversations and to leave it to the reader to grasp their significance. This fundamental technique of satire in the *Ju-lin wai-shih* has distinct rhetorical effects; and since the satirical art is pragmatic, it is proper and fitting that we should give some consideration to these effects.

First of all, the appearance of objectivity, the seeming absence of exaggeration or understatement on the part of the narrator, greatly increases the work's immediacy and believability. Characters in the *Ju-lin wai-shih* are neither oversized monsters like Pantagruel or Gargantua nor fantastic midgets like the Lilliputians; neither do they act out their dullness in some allegorical world. Instead, they come directly from the cities and towns of the Yangtze plain, visit teashops, restaurants, and brothels, transport themselves in boats and carts, eat duck and pork and dumplings, compose poetry, engage in domestic quarrels, attend plays—in sum, they do everything people in the China of their times did in their daily lives. Without having to make the comparison required in works of extended metaphor or allegory, the eighteenth-century Chinese reader would find the society depicted in the *Ju-lin wai-shih* immediately familiar and, without having to make any mental leaps, take the dullness contained therein as identical to that existing in his own world. It is for this reason that, as an early commentator reports, the readers of the novel used to warn their friends to "take care not to read the *Ju-lin wai-shih*; for, if you do, you will feel that among all your relatives and acquaintances, none will remain untainted by it."[38]

Second, this technique of showing rather than telling has the advantage of neutralizing the reader's natural repugnance toward blatant didacticism, toward being told what to think or believe.[39] Without question, the *Ju-lin wai-shih* is geared to instruct, but it does this mostly by artistic persuasion. In dramatizing his message, the narrator subtly manipulates the reader, allowing him to make his own discoveries while maintaining the illusion that whatever conclusions he comes to are indeed his own. No one, least of all the narrator, ever states that Niu Pu-lang is a liar warped by a lust for fame: this is a conclusion left for the reader to make, inevitable though it may be.

Third, it is important to note that by encountering dunce after dunce among the one hundred and eighty-odd characters in the novel, by becoming indignant at their inhumanity or by laughing at their folly, the reader unconsciously moves over to the author's side, accepts his moral premises and, along with them, the pleasurable feeling of superiority over the endless parade of unconscious souls who troop across the novel's pages. Even as he laughs at Fan Chin clutching a chicken by the neck and muttering "I have passed" at the news of his examination success, even as he shakes his head at the geomancers of Wu-ho sniffing at the mud of potential grave sites and chewing it around in their mouths, he has unwittingly agreed with the author that *kung-ming fu-kuei* brings about nothing but indignity, inhumanity, and chaos.

Finally, these three effects—of great immediacy and believability, of the illusion of discovery, and of moral suasion—can combine to produce a fourth: that of self-examination, embarrassment, and self-warning. For even as the reader encounters the thoroughly convincing portraits and scenes, discovers repeatedly the same moral message, and indulges in the initial pleasure of transcendent knowledge and virtue, he soon finds himself wondering whether dullness has not also touched his own soul as it has touched so many others not altogether unlike himself. Has he ever fabricated lies to cover up or to advance himself, as Niu Pu-lang does? Does he also pretend to know when he does not, like Chang Ching-chai? Or does he slight others of inferior status, like Mei Chiu? In general, does he, at least in his own fashion, also seek after *kung-ming fu-kuei*, to the detriment of his humanity and his intellect? As the Hsien-chai lao-jen Preface puts it, among those who read about the dunces in the *Ju-lin wai-shih*, "no matter what their moral character, there is none who would not find himself mirrored in it." In the end, it is this self-mirroring effect which can drag the reader from his superior perch and make him cringe in self-embarrassment.

These effects cannot of course be said to occur with every reader; by listing them, I do not mean to imply that all readers are the same, that they do not approach the *Ju-lin wai-shih* with an infinite range of temperament, intelligence, and background, all of which would affect their conclusions. Nor, indeed, is the work consistently good rhetoric in every episode or character portrayal: its unevenness has been mentioned before. Still, we can say that, for the most part, Wu Ching-tzu's satirical novel shows itself capable of achieving all these effects and that, as rhetorical and didactic literature, it is an impressive work of its kind.

And despite its pragmatic nature, few will deny that it is art. But is it "great art, or good art, or Art"? The answer depends entirely on the ultimately arbitrary premises under which critics have approached literature, and the question will never be settled to everyone's satisfaction. Nevertheless, it is a question too important to ignore. In our next chapter, we shall consider whether Wu Ching-tzu's didacticism detracts from the quality of his literary product by examining what is undeniably a cornerstone of his art: the realism of his narrative.

CHAPTER 5

Realism and Rhetoric

I The Problem of Realism

WHILE the term "realism" has stubbornly remained as a central concept in the criticism of Western fiction, it has never enjoyed a unity of understanding as to its actual meaning. Almost from the moment of its recognition as a characteristic of much of modern (post eighteenth-century) narrative, it has acquired a veritable plethora of qualifications—quotidian realism, subjective realism, formal realism, socialist realism, to name but a few that come immediately to mind—as if, as one writer puts it, critics feel safe to send it out only "under escort" or only "when safely handcuffed by inverted commas."[1] The problem is twofold: no one in modern times can agree on what reality is, and on how art, literary or otherwise, should be related to reality.

It is easy to see that when we apply the term interculturally, namely, in the criticism of Chinese fiction, the problem compounds itself. We can never be sure that Chinese authors perceive reality in ways identical to their Western counterparts; and we are forced to account for the didactic role the Chinese habitually assign to their literary endeavors.

These difficulties have brought on two distinct reactions from Western critics who evaluate Chinese fiction. On the one hand, there are those who ignore the problem altogether and blatantly demand that Chinese fiction be judged by the tenets of Western realism, pure and simple.[2] More recently, one critic has argued the opposite: that realism as we know it is misleading when applied to traditional Chinese fiction, which would be much better understood and appreciated if the idea were discarded altogether.[3]

It seems to me that neither solution is ideal. For, while indiscriminately .stuffing Chinese fiction into Western molds can and

109

does obscure its special merits, discarding realism as a working critical concept effectively separates Chinese fiction from its counterpart in the West and suggests a mutual isolation that is counterproductive and ultimately just as misleading.[4] The better solution, and likely the more accurate one, lies in some middle ground: the insights of Western realism can be useful in the appreciation of Chinese fiction if they are applied with caution, and with the proper qualifications.

II *Didactic Concerns*

Ian Watt has argued, for example, that realism, which defines the Western novel, arose in eighteenth-century Europe, spurred on by philosophies which no longer saw truth and reality in generalities, but which demanded the examination of individual particulars.[5] To this day, whatever a Western critic may mean when he speaks of realism, he seldom goes outside of these same assumptions. And without doubt, it is the agnostic focus on particulars that causes many critics to frown on the heavy doses of didacticism they find in Chinese fiction. As C. T. Hsia puts it, it is didacticism, a general and "extrinsic" concern, which violates realism by exercising what Keats had called "a palpable design" upon the reader, since that design "is incompatible with the full-bodied presentation of reality."[6]

But if reality to the Chinese is, as we have reason to believe, less fragmented, and indeed less mysterious, than to the modern Westerner, then reality's "full-bodied presentation" would not be seen as incompatible with a didactic concern. Unlike Joyce, or James, or Flaubert, the traditional Chinese author does not set out to explore reality. Reality is to him self-evident, and he sets himself up as its *transmitter* rather than as its *discoverer*. Accordingly, he adopts the role of the omniscient and intrusive narrator and presents what is essentially a single point of view, often in an unabashedly sermonizing tone. In contrast to the artistic complexities of Western realistic fiction which, for example, presents dynamically interacting points of view between the narrator and various characters, which delves into individual psyches and plumbs the depths of particular human souls, Chinese fiction (or any didactic fiction) may indeed appear to be simple and even artistically primitive. Those of us who purport to deal with Chinese fiction both traditional and modern are thus led to ask whether its didactic concerns preclude it from becoming accomplished art.

In examining the *Ju-lin wai-shih* as satire, this study attempts to provide a tentative answer, though the problem deserves far more extensive treatment. The reason for using a satirical work is simple: of all modes of literature, satire is the most obviously didactic, the most unabashedly rhetorical, the most concerned with persuading the reader for good and against evil.[7] If we can show that the overriding moral concerns of satirical fiction do not preclude the presence of artistic realism, then we can safely conclude that didacticism and art in literature need not be mutually exclusive.

As satirical fiction, the *Ju-lin wai-shih's* concern is clearly didactic. Our interest here is not this concern per se, but whether a goodly amount of artistic realism can exist alongside of it. Put another way, the question is whether this work, which does not explore particular realities as an aesthetic end, but seeks primarily to convey a general moral truth in a persuasive manner, can also contain the kind of realism we have come to associate with the best of fictional art.

III *Psychological Worlds*

If we were to go by what has been written about the *Ju-lin wai-shih* in the West, the answer could not be an unqualified yes. Oldřich Král, for example, insists that Wu Ching-tzu "intentionally" suppresses any desire to penetrate into his characters' inner consciousness and hesitates to describe the "inner life" of his dunces.[8] C. T. Hsia, writing years later, concurs: ". . . with all his technical contributions to the Chinese novel, Wu shows curiously little ambition to explore that last frontier of fiction, the interior world of consciousness. . . . he remained content to depict the external, visible world even though his sensitive recluses could have become far more interesting if their mental conditions had been fully described."[9] Both Král and Hsia are evidently looking for evidence of an accomplished realism in the *Ju-lin wai-shih*, of which explorations of interior worlds of individuals represent the "last frontier." That they failed to find satisfactory evidence of this in the work can be easily explained: the *Ju-lin wai-shih* is satire and is thus more concerned with rhetoric, with the transmission of a generalized message, than with the disinterested discovery of particularized "truth." On the other hand, their judgment that the depiction of character in the word remains largely on the surface appears somewhat hasty, expecially in light of a careful reading of many passages in the text.

In Chapter 3, for instance, we come across the famous episode of

Chou Chin, who himself had suffered repeated humiliations and
trials before his examination success, encountering Fan Chin, then
still a pitiful, frustrated scholar attending the civil-service examinations over which Chou now presides. We should first note how the
author sets up his didactic point by describing Chou's mental state:
"Now though Chou Chin [as a new examiner] engaged several secretaries, he thought: 'I suffered so long myself in these matters; now
that I'm in office, I should read all the papers carefully rather than
just listen to my secretaries and thus possibly suppress real talent
. . . .' " At the third session, he notices Fan Chin, the last candidate
to enter: ". . . his face was thin and sallow, his beard and sideburns
were flecked with white, a torn felt hat sat on his head. Kwangtung
has a mild climate; still this was the early part of the twelfth month
and the student was still wearing a hempen gown, shivering with
cold as he took his paper and repaired to his cell. Chou Chin made a
mental note of this before sealing up the gates and going inside."
One can of course take this portrait of the luckless Fan Chin as
simple and objective; but the important point is not so much that he
is objectively pitiful, but that he subjectively appears so to Chou
Chin, whose subsequent judgment would then become so much
more comprehensible and convincing to the reader.

Lest we miss the point, the narrator reiterates Fan Chin's sorry
state by making him appear once more in front of Chou:

The man's clothes were so threadbare that a few more holes had appeared
since he went into the cell. Examiner Chou looked at his own garments—
his crimson robe and gilt belt: how magnificent they were! Then he referred
to the register of names and asked the student, "You're Fan Chin?"

Fan Chin knelt down and replied, "Yes, that's me, your undergraduate."

"How old are you this year?"

"My age is written as thirty on the register. Actually I am fifty-four."

"How many times have you taken the examinations?"

"I first sat for them when I was twenty; since then I have taken them over
twenty times."

"How is it that you have never passed?"

"It's always because my compositions are too poor," replied Fan Chin. "So
none of the honorable examiners would grant me the favor of passing me."

"That may not be the only reason," said Examiner Chou. "Leave your
paper here, and I will read it through carefully." Fan kowtowed and went
off.[10]

Indisputably, the account covers little more than outward appearances; and yet these appearances are so structured as to lead the

reader into Chou Chin's mind, so that he can follow Chou's calcula-
tions and grasp the reasons for his decisions. For by now, we can see
that, even before reading Fan's essay, Chou is psychologically predisposed to pass him; so psychologically predisposed, in fact, that
Chou actually talks himself into it. At the first reading, we are told
the essay is nearly unintelligible. By the third reading, however,
Chou convinces himself that it is "the most wonderful essay in the
world—every word a pearl."

IV Rhetorical Realism

Would this type of fiction qualify as "psychological fiction"? A
modern, Western critic would probably think not, but it is important to specify why not. Psychological fiction of a kind which would
satisfy the modern critic would likely conceive of the human mind as
dynamic and unpredictable and would set out to explore its multiple
facets and to follow its constant changes, with no further motive than
the exploration itself. More than likely, the narrator would be a
seeker himself, at least giving the impression that he goes wherever
the mind takes him. While it is less than accurate to say that the
author of the *Ju-lin wai-shih* refrains from entering a character's
inner world, it is nevertheless true that he maintains the omniscient
stance of the traditional storyteller, that he is making the moral
point rather than struggling to discover it. To him, mental states are
largely static and discernible, and he sets out to persuade his readers of what he already knows. Chou Chin's mind is no mystery; the
important thing is merely to lead the reader into it, so that he
becomes persuaded to the same conclusions as the author.

And what would these conclusions be? In the context of this
particular passage, we may say that the civil-service examinations,
which consume the total scholarly energies of such hapless souls as
Fan Chin, are after all so subjectively scored, so utterly dependent
on the personal whim of the examiner, that passing them in no way
proves genuine learning, just as failing them indicates no ignorance.

What realism we find in the account, what minute examination of
an individual mind, is not crafted for itself, but only in order to
advance this argument. For the most part, the author of the *Ju-lin
wai-shih* chooses to show the reader scenes or characters without
direct comment, and critics have praised him for it. It is crucial to
see, however, that this is a rhetorical, rather than a purely aesthetic,
technique: even Chinese readers get tired of being directly told,
and telling is usually less effective than showing. In dramatizing his

message under an objective pose, the author subtly manipulates the reader, allows him to make his own discoveries, while maintaining the illusion that whatever conclusions he comes to are indeed his own. In this way, realism in the *Ju-lin wai-shih* can be seen to work hand in glove with didacticism, drawing its motivation and direction from the author's desire to teach, and making the author's teaching more palatable and convincing.

But can this relationship be a limiting one? Do didactic needs eventually prevent the full development of realism in Chinese fiction? These questions cannot really be answered without a far more extensive study of all kinds of Chinese fictional narrative, both traditional and modern. In the case of the *Ju-lin wai-shih* though, we can answer that the author, because of (rather than in spite of) his didactic concern, is clearly probing beneath surfaces and beyond stereotypes, and evincing in his character portrayals an impressive understanding of human psychology. Nowhere is this clearer than in the novel's accounts of dreams.

V *Dream Episodes*

For the critic in search of psychological realism in any work of fiction, the dream episode becomes a most useful piece of evidence, since it shows whether the work is oriented toward romance or toward more realistic depiction. In the *Ju-lin wai-shih*, the author evidently cannot resist including romantic elements in at least one dream. In Chapter 2, Wang Hui, already a metropolitan graduate, meets the young student Hsun Mei and reveals a dream, he had in which he saw both their names on the same list of successful examination candidates. In Chapter 7, this improbable dream is shown essentially to come true. Much more typically, however, dreams in the *Ju-lin wai-shih* fulfill a more realistic role; they convey a character's state of mind and reveal the author's understanding of psychological realities. It is this understanding that advances the rhetorical power of the work. Consider the following three examples.

At the welcoming banquet for Chou Chin previously examined, Mei Chiu, at one point, abruptly turns to the subject of dreams "with his mouth full of cake":

"Mr. Chou,[" he asked Chou Chin,"] these past years, during the examinations, what dreams have you had?"

"Why, none at all," Chou replied.

"I was fortunate," said Mei Chiu. "Last year on New Year's Day, I dreamed that I was on a very high mountain. The sun directly above me fell right down on my head! It frightened me so I broke out in a sweat! After I woke up, I touched my head and could still feel some heat. At the time I didn't know what it meant. But now that I think about it, what an accurate sign that was!"[11]

Here our satirist has led us into the mind of a dunce, who becomes another ludicrous example of the pride of status in a competitive society. Whether this dream-fantasy actually occurred or not is irrelevant; the dream is not recorded for itself, but only to reveal the dreamer as a despicable braggart, all puffed up from what is ultimately a minor achievement. With this added detail, the satirist reinforces the distaste the reader should already feel for Mei and for the social system which has produced him.

The overexuberant tone in which Mei describes his dream may seem somewhat exaggerated (as much of satire is exaggerated). But this detracts little from the realistic understanding the author evidently has of a cocky youth too big for his britches, and the ability he possesses to convey this understanding with artistic indirection. Wu Ching-tzu's fundamental grasp of human psychology is again evident in our next example, taken from the beginning of Chapter 16. In the midst of the masterfully crafted story of Kuang Chao-jen, the author has Kuang's mother describe her dreams to her son on his homecoming:

"Since you left with that merchant over a year ago," she told him, "I've not had a moment of peace. One night I dreamed you had fallen into the water, and I woke up crying. One night I dreamed you had broken your leg. One night I dreamed that there was a big growth on your face; you showed it to me and I tried to tear it off with my hand, but I just couldn't. One night I dreamed you came home and stood before me in tears; and then I cried too until I woke myself up. One night I saw you in a gauze cap and heard you had become an official. I laughed and said, 'How can country folk like us become officials?'

"Then a man there told me: 'This official is not your son. Your son, however, also became an official; but he will never come back to you any more.'

"That made me cry again and I said: 'If I shan't be able to see him again once he becomes an official, I'd rather he didn't become one.' "[12]

We can see here that the author never lets go of his didactic point: as everywhere in the novel, he continues to impress upon the reader the natural antagonism between official success on the one hand and true learning and humanity on the other. The anxiety of a mother fretting over the well-being of her son is conveyed by descriptions of her dreams, which attract the reader's sympathy by appealing both to his emotions and to his intellect because of the judicious use of realistic detail. By listening to her dreams, we understand her love for her son; when we later see that this love is betrayed by her son's worldly success which alters his originally good character, we are moved in recalling the intended irony of her words: "If I shan't be able to see him again once he becomes an official, I'd rather he didn't become one."

This kind of rhetorical realism constitutes the most significant feature of Wu Ching-tzu's art: the satire in the novel is effective because its moral point is convincingly argued; and its moral point is convincingly argued ultimately because the author possesses the intellectual ability to fathom the human psyche and the artistic ability to convey his insights with realistic detail.

Of course the dreams we have been examining, which display this kind of realistic detail on the one hand, are also terse and indirect on the other. It is as if the author is unsure or unwilling to linger for long in a character's mind. In the entire novel, only one dream is described directly and presented in complete detail. This is the dream of Pin-niang, the courtesan who is consumed by a passion for wealth and fame. As one of the very best examples of rhetorical realism in the *Ju-lin wai-shih*, this dream certainly deserves more attention than critics have hitherto accorded it.

VI *Pin-niang's Dream*

As with so many of the best constructed episodes in the novel, this dream is carefully prefaced with details which add to its plausibility. Pin-niang first spends the day entertaining Chen Mu-nan (Ch'en Mu-nan), the personal friend of a duke, bestowing her favors on him because she sees in him a chance to advance her own position. Enchanted by her charms, Chen tells her that he will buy her from her mistress and take her with him to his official post. At this, Pin-niang falls rapturously into his arms and calls on the gods to witness his words. They make love, and later Pin-niang falls asleep beside her guest, to be startled by the sputtering of the lamp wick as the third watch (that is, midnight) is sounded outside. She checks to be sure that Chen is fast asleep and, tucking the quilt around him, dozes off again.

She had slept for some time when she heard a gonging outside.
"It's after midnight," she thought. "What are gongs doing outside our door?"
The gongs came closer and closer, and someone outside announced: "Your ladyship, will you please proceed to your post?"
Throwing an embroidered jacket over her shoulders, with her slippers only half on, Pin-niang hurried out. Four maids-in-waiting met her outside, each kneeling on both knees and saying, "The fourth Mr. Chen has gone to his post as prefect of Hang-chou. He has sent us to escort your ladyship there to share his wealth and splendor."
On hearing this, Pin-niang hastened back to her room to comb her hair and put on her outer garments. The maids handed her a phoenix crown and a cape of embroidered clouds, and she put them on. A large palanquin was waiting outside the hall, and into this she stepped. Once carried outside the gate, she saw a whole procession of gongs, penants, parasols, musicians, and attendants. "Carry her to the palace," she heard someone say.
Just as they were proceeding triumphantly, a sallow-faced nun with a shaven head stepped forward from the side of the road and laid hold of Pin-niang inside the palanquin. "This is my disciple!" the nun shouted at the attendants. "Where are you taking her off to?"
"I am the official wife of the perfect of Hang-chou." protested Pin-niang. "How dare you seize me, you bald-headed nun!"
She was going to order the attendants to lock up the nun when, looking around, she saw that they had disappeared! She cried out in her dismay and bumped into Chen Mu-nan, then woke to discover that it had all been a dream.[13]

Despite the continued use of the third-person narrative, it is evident that the entire dream is rendered from Pin-niang's point of view and represents a direct entrance into her mind: all the words and actions recorded are actually her thoughts. But these thoughts, as detailed and realistic as they are, are not put together for the sake of realism alone. Above all, they are designed to reveal in a thoroughly convincing manner the internal workings of yet another mind poisoned by the drive for wealth and status, so that the reader may be instructed and warned. Here is a nearly perfect example of how artistic realism and didactic morality work together: the reader becomes convinced because the rhetoric is so real.

From what occurs prior to the dream itself, we can see how the dream comes about. Pin-niang showers her favors on Chen in hopes of becoming an official's lady. These hopes are raised to a high pitch when Chen tells her about his impending official appointment and promises to make her his concubine. In her excited state, Pin-niang is unable to sleep soundly so that even the sputter of a burning wick can wake her. Entirely naturally, she acts out her desires in a dream based on all these facts. In her dream, the attainment of official status is linked directly to images of fancy clothes, of gongs and maids-in-waiting, of "penants, parasols, musicians, and attendants" clustering around a palanquin—flights of fancy which reveal realistically her status-loving character, her rather superficial tastes, her currently excited frame of mind. They also reveal her insecurities, and the sallow-faced nun who appears to drag her away in her moment of fulfillment is the embodiment of her darkest fears. It is the presence of these fears which makes Pin-niang such a human figure; even as the reader sees her flaws, he cannot help but understand and sympathize with her plight, while taking warning himself about the consequences of misdirected ambition.

This masterful episode, along with others cited in this chapter, should demonstrate that realism in fiction need not occur only in the absence of a didactic "palpable design." If many didactic works do lack a satisfactory measure of realistic art, it is likely because their creators were too eager to present their moral doctrines to do so with design or subtlety or well-chosen details. In contrast, Wu Ching-tzu had enough artistic patience and sophistication to present his moral views with a certain witty indirection, and the result is a happy one for both his doctrines and his art.

CHAPTER 6

Wu Ching-tzu and Chinese Fiction

IN eighteenth-century China, as Wu Ching-tzu wrote the *Ju-lin wai-shih*, popular vernacular fiction continued to be held in low regard even though, to a large degree, it had already been taken over by members of the lettered class. In the dominant Confucian point of view, literature was a serious, almost sacred, business, undertaken for no lesser purpose than the betterment of society. Vernacular fiction up to that time cannot be said to be amoral, even if it sometimes contradicts in its plots the explicit moral pronouncements of its narrators.[1] Yet, until the *Ju-lin wai-shih*, vernacular fiction's basic characteristic was not moralistic. Rather, in both form—direct, unsophisticated, exhaustive—and content—sensational, romantic, comical—it directed itself to the amusement of the reader, on whom it placed little or no demand. We know that serious litterateurs were sometimes addicted to it; but they read it casually, and for fun rather than for edification.

This was so even though, in the two centuries before Wu Ching-tzu, highly educated men like Wu Ch'eng-en (ca. 1500–1582) and Feng Meng-lung (1574–1646) lent their considerable literary talents to the editing, compiling, and writing of popular fiction. It was as if the genre, by nature, was expected to entertain, and those who worked in it deliberately molded their art to this expectation.

It is true that, in certain works, the spirit of frivolity is not unmixed with a certain amount of seriousness. Stories of exemplary morality in Feng's collection, such as "Wu Pao-an ch'i-chia shu yu" ("Wu Pao-an Abandons His Family to Ransom a Friend") or "Fan Chü-ch'ing chi-shu ssu-sheng chiao" ("Fan Chü-ch'ing Seals Eternal Friendship with Chicken and Millet") constitute one kind of example; the anonymous Ming novel *Chin P'ing Mei*, which examines to some extent the realities of rivalry and manipulation in a complex domestic situation, is another.[2] Wu Ching-tzu, however, goes much

119

further, and his work marks a fundamental development in the direction of the tradition.

As we have seen, Wu did adopt and follow the conventions of popular fiction, retaining many of its formulaic features, even imitating one of its plots; his narrative also has a clearly entertaining Side. Yet his novel is the first to evince a fundamental and profound didacticism: it advances in a sustained way a doctrine of idealistic Confucianism, and, in keeping with this, it does so with a subtle and sophisticated wit which demands for its full appreciation an alert and cultivated mind. With Wu Ching-tzu, Chinese fiction completes its journey from folksy gossip to refined and serious art, essentially identical to the art of the learned and the leisured. With historical hindsight, we can see that, after Wu Ching-tzu, it would have been only a matter of time before Chinese fiction would have achieved at home the respect it now enjoys, even if China had somehow remained isolated and Confucian.

At about the same time that Wu Ching-tzu was completing the *Ju-lin wai-shih* in the south, his fellow southerner Ts'ao Hsüeh-ch'in was putting together in the northern capital of Peking another work of vernacular fiction destined to become the most acclaimed piece of writing in all of Chinese literature: the *Hung-lou meng* or *Red Chamber Dream.* It has been written, correctly, that this masterwork "provides in one volume a summation of the three-thousand-year span of Chinese literary civilization," including in its pages "a sampling of all the major modes . . . and genres" of Chinese literature.[3] In its complex demonstration of a fairly simple philosophical theme, the illusoriness and mutability of human existence, it displays such a dazzling array of literary characteristics that to place it in any one category would prove unsatisfactory.[4] In his own commentary prefixed to most editions of his novel, Ts'ao Hsüeh-ch'in mentions the "shame and remorse" brought on by the repeated failures of his life and his desire to make a record of the female companions of his opulent youth "when I dressed in silk and ate delicately." He writes that such a memorial to "those slips of girls" who were superior in every way could "at one and the same time serve as a source of harmless entertainment and as a warning to those who were in the same predicament as myself but who were still in need of awakening."[5] In the space of a short treatise, therefore, we find the author justifying his work as a self-confession, as private history, as entertainment, and as didactic literature. Indeed, just as the *Red Chamber Dream* is encyclopedic in content, it is universal in appeal; critics of all biases and persuasions have echoed its praises to our day, and for an astonishing variety of reasons. It is precisely this comprehensiveness that separates the *Red Chamber Dream* from the *Ju-lin wai-shih*. Together, they mark the eighteenth century as the time when the Chinese novel became truly refined and self-conscious, the time when the co-optation of a genre of folk art by the intellectual aristocracy was completed. But, separately, each can be seen to branch out and form a subtradition of its own, the *Ju-lin wai-shih* taking on the relatively narrow didactic burdens of classical literature, and the *Red Chamber Dream* the broader amalgamation of all facets of China's literary and philosophical culture.

As a novel that stirred countless imaginations, the *Red Chamber Dream* did not lack imitations and sequels; but the high standards it set were never approached and its subtradition never grew. The subtradition that began with the *Ju-lin wai-shih*, however, has flourished and proliferated ever since, first with the highly didactic "late Ch'ing" novels of the nineteenth century, then with the socially conscious "modern" fiction of the 1920s and 1930s. In more recent times, this subtradition easily slipped into Marxist garb, its didactic and moralistic nature intact even as it now wags its critical finger at imperialism and class exploitation, as well as, incidentally, the Confucianism its early predecessor so staunchly upholds.

The main reasons for this are clearly historical. Since the troubles which began in the 1840s, the Opium War, large-scale foreign encroachment, repeated national defeats and humiliations, domestic rebellion and unrest, and finally revolution, Chinese authors have not known the cultural self-confidence and the sense of national security both Wu Ching-tzu and Ts'ao Hsüeh-ch'in enjoyed. Wu Ching-tzu wrote didactic fiction because his own nature and upbringing inclined him that way; his values are understandably conservative. More recent authors became didactic because the stresses of the times made them take up the pen as a weapon against social and political ills; their values are accordingly revolutionary. In regards to the fiction both Wu and these authors produced, the question remains whether the overriding desire to instruct, the "palpable design" in their works, constitutes a barrier to genuine artistic achievement. In comparison to Ts'ao Hsüeh-ch'in, Wu Ching-tzu's artistic vision may indeed be seen to be narrowed by his didacticism. But, from this study, it should be evident that didacticism has been more of a boon than a bane to his brand of art. By understanding and appreciating Wu Ching-tzu, we can begin also to understand and appreciate the many who followed in his footsteps, and, in the process, broaden our recognition of the possibilities of human artistic creativity.

Texts of the Ju-lin wai-shih

How old Chinese novels came to be the way they are today is usually a puzzlement to, and a source of unending debate among, modern scholars. For, unlike the vast majority of novels in the West, which can be dated and attributed to an author or authors and which deviate little from edition to edition, traditional Chinese novels are often the evolved product of many hands and are likely to come in a bewildering array of versions. Compared to such novels as *Water Margin, Journey to the West,* or *Golden Lotus,* however, the *Ju-lin wai-shih* has only a few textual problems, and only one of these matters much in the long run.

Modern scholarship has been able to establish Wu Ching-tzu as the novel's only author of consequence and to determine that some form of the first text, as a manuscript, existed as early as 1748–1750. We are also fairly certain that this text was published between 1768 and 1779, even though the earliest extant edition dates only to 1803.[1] Speculation that the work took shape some time between 1735 and 1745 cannot be far wrong, despite the absence of hard evidence. And enough uniformity exists in all the extant editions to make textual investigation a rather academic matter. Nevertheless, some interesting questions (as well as one crucial one) are still unanswered, and I summarize them here not to settle them but only to stimulate further discussion.

I *Important Extant Texts*

Of all the texts of the *Ju-lin wai-shih* now extant in China and the rest of the world, the following thirteen are the most important.[2]

1803 Wo-hsien ts'ao-t'ang edition. A small (only 128 millimeters long and 95 wide) "handbook" size text with traditional Chinese double pages, each containing nine lines, eighteen characters to a line. Anonymous but sometimes insightful commentary appears after each chapter. A preface by Hsien-chai lao-jen is dated 1736, though most scholars would not accept this date as the later limit of the novel. In 1975, the Jen-min wen-hsüeh ch'u-pan she of Peking published a slightly enlarged photolithographic reproduction of this text (see Chapter 2, note 7).

1816 Yi-ku t'ang edition. A woodblock edition similar in appearance to the text above, complete with the Hsien-chai lao-jen preface. This text served as the basis for the first Ya-tung edition of 1920.

1869 Ch'ün-yü chai edition. A much larger text that does not otherwise differ from the 1803 Wo-hsien edition; the new format has nine lines to a page, twenty large characters to a line. A copy is preserved in the Tōyō Bunko in Tokyo.

1869 Su-chou shu-chü edition. This text is so similar to the Ch'ün-yü chai text above that they have been taken to be the same. The only difference appears to be the addition of Chin Ho's important postscript, dated "winter, the tenth month of the eighth year in the reign of T'ung-chih" or November–December, 1869. A somewhat shorter and different version of this postscript appears in many subsequent editions, but the version here seems to be the most reliable.

1874 First Shen-pao kuan (Shanghai news) edition. A popular typeset edition published in Shanghai and clearly based on the 1803 Wo-hsien text; it also contains Chin Ho's postscript as well as "explanatory notes" by Chang Wen-hu (1808–1885), the author of the *Ju-lin wai-shih p'ing* (see below) who writes under the name of T'ien-mu shan ch'iao.

1874 Ch'i-hsing t'ang tseng-ting (supplemented) edition. This text contains a new preface, signed with the pseudonym Hsing-yüan t'ui-shih.

1881 Second Shen-pao kuan edition. Essentially the same text as the first Shen-pao kuan edition, except that it is footnoted throughout with Chang Wen-hu's commentary.

1914 Yü-wen shu-chü and Hai-tso shu-chü edition. This text contains yet another new preface, signed by Hsi-hung-sheng and dated 1888.

1920 Ya-tung t'u-shu kuan edition. Based on the 1816 Yi-ku t'ang edition, this text is the first really modern edition; edited and punctuated by Wang Yüan-fang, who includes the disputed Chapter 56 as an epilogue.

1922 Ya-tung t'u-shu kuan ssu-pan (fourth printing) edition. This text was completely reedited by Wang Yüan-fang, who was dissatisfied with his own earlier work. It includes Hu Shih's two studies of Wu Ching-tzu's life, modern prefaces by Ch'en Tu-hsiu (1879–1943) and Ch'ien Hsüan-t'ung (1887–1938), the Hsien-chai lao-jen preface, Chin Ho's postscript, the Hsing-yüan t'ui-shih preface, as well as special notes by the editor.

1937 Shang-wu yin-shu kuan (Commercial Press) edition. In all likelihood, this is a modernized version of the 1881 second Shen-pao kuan edition. It contains Chin Ho's postscript and both the commentary and the notes of Chang Wen-hu.

1954 Tso-chia ch'u-pan she edition. A completely faithful reprinting in modern type of the 1803 Wo-hsien edition, including even the latter's mistakes. Notations are relatively sparse, and simplified characters are not used. This is the text that has been reprinted by various publishers in Hong Kong.

1958 Jen-min wen-hsüeh ch'u-pan she edition. The editor, Chang Hui-chien, carefully corrected what he considered to be mistakes in the 1803 Wo-hsien text, added very detailed notation, and produced a modernistic version complete with simplified characters and a Western design which includes horizontal lines, pages which open from right to left, and illustrations by the popular artist Ch'eng Shih-fa. But because Chang does not indicate exactly where in the text he made his corrections, the 1954 Tso-chia text is more reliable for scholarly purposes.

The one point of serious contention among modern scholars regarding the most authoritative text of the *Ju-lin wai-shih* has to do with the novel's actual length. Variously, it is said to contain sixty, fifty-six, fifty-five, and fifty *hui* or *chüan* (which I, for the sake of convenience, call "chapters").

II *The Sixty-Chapter Problem*

Aside from the editions listed above, none of which contains more than fifty-six chapters, another edition exists which is in sixty chapters. In 1888, the Ch'i-hsing t'ang, which fourteen years earlier had produced a reedited fifty-six chapter *Ju-lin wai-shih* with a new

preface, came forth with a *tseng-pu* ("added and restored") edition
with yet another new preface (by Hsi-hung-sheng, later included in
the 1914 Yü-wen and Hai-tso edition) and four additional chapters
on top of the slightly abridged original material. These new chapters
were inserted into the latter part of the novel (after Chapter 42),
thus expanding it to a full sixty chapters.[3] This kind of interpolation
is not at all uncommon among traditional Chinese booksellers eager
to capitalize on the commercial success of a particular work. In this
case, however, the job was done so poorly that the new version
never took on the popularity of the original, and scholars have uni-
versally dismissed the additions as fraudulent. Externally, the
sixty-chapter version contradicts the word of both Ch'eng Chin-fang
and Chin Ho that the original *Ju-lin wai-shih* contains either fifty or
fifty-five chapters. And internally, the relatively lewd and
superstitious content of the four added chapters diverges markedly
from the general impression the novel gives of a morally upright
work free of supernatural concern.[4] Indeed, no one seems to have
taken this long version seriously enough to bother to study the four
added chapters carefully for inconsistencies. Since Hu Shih's serious
studies of the *Ju-lin wai-shih*, few sixty-chapter versions have been
printed, and we may agree with Liu Ts'un-yan that the new material
is the interpolated work of "some later busybody" and not worthy of
serious attention.[5]

III   *The Fifty-Six Chapter Problem and the Fifty-Five Chapter Problem*

Since the problems of whether the original version of the *Ju-lin
wai-shih* contains fifty-five or fifty-six chapters are interlinked, it is
best to discuss them together. The 1803 Wo-hsien edition and all
extant editions of the *Ju-lin wai-shih* listed in Sun K'ai-ti's *Catalogue
of Popular Chinese Fiction* (with the exception, of course, of the
sixty-chapter edition discussed above) contain fifty-six chapters.[6]
Most modern editions, such as the two from Ya-tung t'u-shu kuan,
include Chapter 56 either in the main body or as an appendix. Yet
the preponderance of current scholarly opinion holds this final chapter to be a later addition, but the reasons adduced for this are
flimsier than we might expect. Chin Ho's postscript to the 1869
Su-chou edition includes the following remarks near the end:

Books authored by the Master [Wu Ching-tzu] are all in odd numbers [of
chüan]. The original edition of this book contains only fifty-five *chüan*,

ending after the account of the four gentlemen of the harp, chess, calligraphy, and painting which leads to the lyric "Ch'in-yüan ch'un." Someone,
sometime, recklessly added a "yu-pang" (posthumous examination register)
chüan, rearranging parallel prose from the collection of the Master's essays
to form official proclamations in an inferior and contemptible way. We
should now delete it and restore the work to its original form.[7]

The earliest extensive commentary on the *Ju-lin wai-shih*, the 1885
Ju-lin wai-shih p'ing (*Commentary*) of Chang Wen-hu includes an
abridged version of this postscript and concurs with its position on
the unreliability of Chapter 56.[8] Chang argues from what he per-
ceives as internal evidence that the "yu-pang" chapter does not fit
the author's intention: "The 'yu-pang' chapter is a forced summary,
and much of it really does not fit the work. The author's intention is
to provide no answer as the answer, to conclude vaguely. Why must
one add this extraneous material? The Chin Ho postscript takes it to
be an uncouth continuation to a beautiful work of art [*huang-ts'ang
hsü tiao*]. How true! How true!"[9]

While it is true that most of this chapter is not satirical but, on the
contrary, sanctifies with little justification many characters who
were criticized in the novel proper, Chang's argument is still not
convincing. For the four eccentrics clearly affirm the author's ideology and express his ultimate hope. So even if Wu Ching-tzu does
end his story with Chapter 55, the ending is anything but vague,
and it provides a definite answer to the social and moral problems
the book presents. Nevertheless, like Chang, most modern scholars
have accepted Chin Ho's word and consider the "yu-pang" chapter
extraneous and not genuine. Neither the two authoritative texts
produced in the People's Republic of China in the 1950s nor the
English translation of 1957 include Chapter 56. On the other hand,
following Chin·Ho's recommendation, they all conclude Chapter 55
with the lyric to the tune "Ch'in-yüan ch'un" which, in the early
editions, is found only in the discarded fifty-sixth chapter.

The question is surely not as settled as most people would believe. Chin Ho wrote his postscript well over a century after Wu
Ching-tzu's death and, while he was related to Wu's family and can
claim some inside knowledge, he provides no proof to support his
assertions. Chin does not, for example, specify which of Wu Ching-
tzu's classical prose compositions was lifted and rearranged to make
up the official documents in the disputed chapter; in fact, he does
not even assure us that he has seen the originals. Furthermore,
Chin's statement that Wu's works all contain an odd number of

chüan is belied by concrete evidence. The extant *Wen-mu shan-fang chi* is in four *chüan* and Ch'eng Chin-fang, Wu Ching-tzu's close acquaintance, has written that the original *Ju-lin wai-shih* was in fifty *chüan*. The contemporary scholar Liu Ts'un-yan has also pointed out that, despite Chin's advice to delete, all the old editions which contain his postscript nevertheless continue to include the fifty-sixth chapter. To Liu, this shows that even though Chin may be correct, he was not able to provide enough evidence to convince later publishers to follow his instructions.[10] Many modern editions also hedge by including the "yu-pang" chapter as an epilogue or as an appendix.

In the absence of concrete evidence of any kind, we can still make a case for the retention, if not for the authenticity, of this much maligned chapter. For contrary to Chang Wen-hu's opinion, the chapter *can* be seen as a fitting and proper conclusion to the novel as a whole. Ho Man-tzu and Chao Ching-shen have pointed out that "yu-pang," which awards posthumous examination titles to fifty-five of the novel's major heroes, corresponds nicely to the incident in the opening chapter in which Wang Mien sees one hundred and ten little stars falling to the southeast as a heavenly sign for the maintenance of China's scholarly fortunes. This correspondence, moreover, would complete the *Ju-lin wai-shih*'s borrowing from the plot of the *Water Margin*, a point discussed earlier in this study.[11] For the *Water Margin* too concludes with the conferral of posthumous imperial honors on the bandit heroes.[12]

Further, Ho makes a good point when he writes that this "yu-pang" chapter is not entirely without the subtle irony that characterizes some of the novel's most outstanding passages. The chapter begins by noting that, many years after all the heroes have passed from the scene, "after the land was long pacified, the emperor held no audience with his ministers all year, every province was wracked by disasters or drought or flood, and refugees lined the roads. Even though the provincial governors memorialized to the court, no one knows whether the emperor's eyes have seen the memorials or not." Then, suddenly, the following imperial decree is issued from the grand secretariat: "In the forty years or so since We ascended the throne, We have been diligent both day and night, not taking time even to eat, because We wish to advance the fortunes of the people . . . to honor and utilize human talent. . . . Presently, there should be no men of wisdom and virtue occupying a lowly status.

But if this is so, why are We not achieving the glory of the Golden Age?"[13] The ironic contrasts in these two juxtaposed passages reveal a style of satire not unlike that found in the novel proper, where verbal claims are often allowed to be undermined by factual descriptions. The land is said to be pacified, but disasters and refugees are everywhere; the emperor has not held court for a year and reads no memorials, but his decree claims a constant diligence which prevents his even taking time out for meals. And in the midst of national disasters, he is blithely wondering why his reign has failed to achieve the glories of the past. To Ho Man-tzu, this style of satire can only be the product of someone with the literary skill of a Wu Ching-tzu, and at any rate, should be preserved. For, ultimately, the "yu-pang" chapter can be seen to present a final irony: that even in death, the literati cannot escape the system of examination honors which dominated their lives.[14]

Finally, there is the content of the chapter itself, the greater part of which is made up of official documents and proclamations, quoted verbatim in very difficult, erudite, and allusive classical Chinese. If someone other than Wu Ching-tzu wrote it, then that person was not unlearned and, judging from some of the sentiments expressed—a love of Nanking and the Yangtze plain, lamentations for the plight of scholars—either knew Wu intimately or was in remarkable accord with his feelings. If, as Chin Ho claims on the other hand, the forger largely rearranged some of Wu's own compositions, then we can say that he did not really do such a poor job of it, and that the chapter would have some definite value, since it would therefore be the repository of one or more of the author's compositions not extant anywhere else.

In any case, the disputed fifty-sixth chapter is not necessarily a misfit, and, I fear, it has been dismissed too hastily on the word of just one man.

IV *The Fifty-Chapter Problem*

The position, first taken in modern times by Hu Shih, that the *Ju-lin wai-shih* originally contained only fifty chapters also comes ultimately from a single source, Ch'eng Chin-fang. In his biography of Wu Ching-tzu, Ch'eng states that Wu, "in imitation of the people of the T'ang dynasty," wrote the novel in fifty *chüan* which "thoroughly explores the world of the literati" and "people competed with each other to circulate and copy it."[15] Hu Shih and

others have also cited the bibliography in the Ch'üan-chiao gazetteer, which lists the *Ju-lin wai-shih* as consisting of fifty *chüan*.[16]
This gazetteer's brief account of Wu's life, however, refers to
Ch'eng Chin-fang's biography as its only source, while two lines out
of a total of eight are nearly verbatim repetitions of Ch'eng's own
words.[17] The likelihood, therefore, is that, in listing the *Ju-lin wai-
shih* as consisting of fifty chapters, the Ch'üan-chiao gazetteer is
merely following Ch'eng Chin-fang, whose account then remains
the sole piece of external evidence supporting the fifty-chapter position.

In his *Catalogue*, Sun K'ai-ti quotes the *Ch'iao-hsi tsa-chi (Miscellaneous Notes West of the Bridge)* of Yeh Ming-feng (1811–1859)
as evidence for the existence of a fifty-chapter version of the *Ju-lin
wai-shih* between the reigns of Tao-kuang and Hsien-feng (about
1851), the time of Yeh's writing.[18] But Yeh's terse, three-line reference to the subject can easily be shown to be no more than a slight
rearrangement of sentences in Ch'eng Chin-fang's biography of Wu,
which Yeh also mentions. Likewise, all references I have seen to the
Ju-lin wai-shih being in fifty *chüan* are verbatim or nearly verbatim
copies of Ch'eng's account.[19] In all probability, therefore, Ch'eng
Chin-fang becomes the sole authority for all those who subscribe to
the fifty-chapter edition. Seen in this light, Hu Shih's position that
the orginal version of the *Ju-lin wai-shih* contained only fifty chapters and the extant texts all include five to six chapters of interpolated materials grows considerably weaker.[20]

Nevertheless, Ch'eng Chin-fang's claim should be taken seriously
since, as a personal friend of the author, he is likely to have had
access to the original copy of the manuscript. Moreover, sudden
shifts in the quality and tone of some of the *Ju-lin wai-shih*'s later
chapters indicate the likely presence of interpolated material. As
stated earlier in this study, this is the one crucial textual problem
that remains unanswered, and the solution of this problem may well
influence the final evaluation of Wu Ching-tzu's art.

Notes and References

Older Chinese texts, whether in the original or in a modern reprint, are referred to by two sets of numerals with a virgule in the middle. The set to the left of the virgule indicates *chüan* or traditional Chines "volume"; that to the right indicates the page number. Where letters *a* and *b* appear with the page number, they refer respectively to the verso and the recto of the page.

Chapter One

1. See the second of his eight lyrics written to the tune of "Mu-lan hua" (abbreviated form) in the *Wen-mu shan-fang chi*, 4/2b, in which he speaks with evident pride concerning the skill he acquired as a composer of dramatic lyrics.

2. Scholars usually trace the term *hsiao-shuo* to a passage in the *Chuang Tzu* (in no. 4 of the *tsa-p'ien*, or "miscellaneous chapters"), a book of Taoist philosophy dating to the fourth or third century B.C. My translation of it is intended to be general without taking into account its various shifts of meaning over the centuries. For a recapitulation of the origins and evolution of the term, see Lu Hsün (Chou Shu-jen), *A Brief History of Chinese Fiction*, 2d ed., trans. Yang Hsien-yi and Gladys Yang (Peking, 1964), pp. 1–9.

3. These are the last four lines of a poem about Wu Ching-tzu written between 1748 and 1750 by Ch'eng Chin-fang and included in *chüan* 2, entitled "Ch'un-fan chi" or "Spring sails collection," of his *Mien-hsing t'ang shih chi (Poetry Collection of the Hall of Positive Conduct)* in twenty-five *chüan* and published in 1818. The poem is reprinted in Ho Tse-han, *Ju-lin wai-shih jen-wu pen-shih k'ao-lüeh* (hereafter cited as Ho Tse-han), p. 188.

4. Leonard Feinberg's book, *The Satirist* (Ames, Iowa, 1965), contains many examples of such attempts.

5. Chang Chung-li, *The Chinese Gentry* (Seattle, 1955), pp. 3–70, explains the many levels of the Chinese civil service examination system in the Ch'ing dynasty. A *lin-sheng* (Chang romanizes it as *ling-sheng*) was a government student *(sheng-yüan* or *hsiu-ts'ai)* who achieved outstanding results in examinations held once every three years by the provincial direc-

tor of studies and thus earned a stipend amounting to an average of four taels per annum. See Chang, pp. 17–18.

6. For an explanation of the terms *chin-shih* and *han-lin*, see Chang Chung-li, pp. 120–24.

7. Lu Chi (261–303) and Lu Yün (262–303), who lived in the Tsin dynasty, were brothers known, among other things, for their literary talent. Likewise, Su Shih (better known as Su Tung-p'o, 1037–1101) and Su Ch'e (1039–1112) were siblings in one of the most renowned literary families of the Northern Sung dynasty.

8. A *mou* is equivalent to less than one sixth of an acre.

9. *Wen-mu shan-fang chi*, 1/6b-7a.

10. Ibid., 1/7a.

11. The original of this work was estimated by Hu Shih to have been published around 1741 and financed largely by Wu Ching-tzu's friend Fang Tsun. Later, it was published again by Shanghai's Ya-tung t'u-shu kuan in June, 1931, in an edition which includes Hu Shih's studies of Wu Ching-tzu as well as a special preface. Still later, the Ku-tien wen-hsüeh ch'u-pan she, Shanghai, produced another edition. Ho Tse-han has pointed out that a much larger collection of Wu's poetry and prose (in twelve *chüan*) was also called the *Wen-mu shan-fang chi*; this latter collection, now lost, is the one referred to in Chin Ho's postscript and various other places and should not be confused with the work cited here. See Ho Tse-han, pp. 178–79, and see section XI of this chapter.

12. Included in the *Hu Shih wen-ts'un*, vol. 2, *chüan* 4, pp. 1–50.

13. Wu Ching-tzu's friend Yen Ch'ang-ming has left a poem describing the lovely natural surroundings of this residence; the poem has been reprinted in Ho Tse-han, p. 190. For Yen's relationship to Wu, see Chang Hui-chien, "Wu Ching-tzu chiao-yu k'ao" in *Ming-Ch'ing hsiao-shuo yenchiu lün-wen chi*, pp. 361–62. Chang, however, confuses the Wen-mu shan-fang residence with Wu's "river house" *(ho-fang)* in Nanking. Wu's *tzu* of Min-hsüan is widely known and referred to in many places. His *hao* of Li-min is a recent discovery from a seal he affixed to an extant specimen of his calligraphy. See Wang Wei-lin, "Ts'ung liang-pu shih-chi-li so chien-tao ti yu-kuan Wu Ching-tzu ti tzu-liao" in *Wen-hsüeh yi-ch'an tseng-k'an*, vol. 11, p. 176. The *hao* of Ch'in-huai yü-k'o appears in a newly discovered preface. See Ch'en Ju-heng, "Wu Ching-tzu *Wen-mu shan-fang chi* wai yi-wen ti fa-hsien" ("The Discovery of a Wu Ching-tzu Composition Outside of the *Wen-mu shan-fang chi*"), in *Wen-hsüeh yi-ch'an hsüan-chi (Selected Essays from Literary Heritage)*, vol. 3 (Peking, 1957), p. 212.

14. For information on these three reigns, see Edwin O. Reischauer and John K. Fairbank, *East Asia: The Great Tradition* (Cambridge, 1960), pp. 345–93; Frederick Wakeman, Jr., "High Ch'ing: 1683–1839", in James B. Crowley, ed., *Modern East Asia: Essays in Interpretation* (New York, 1970), pp. 1–28; Albert Feuerwerker, *State and Society in Eighteenth-Century China: The Ch'ing Empire in Its Glory*, Michigan Papers in

Chinese Studies, no. 27, (Ann Arbor, 1976). See Inada Takashi, "Jurin gaishi no sakusha to jidai" ("The Author and the Times of the *Ju-lin wai-shih*"), in *Chūgoku no hachi dai shōsetsu*, pp. 283–91, and Hu Nien-yi, "Wu Ching-tzu ho t'a ti shih-tai" ("Wu Ching-tzu and His Times"), in *Wen-hsüeh yi-ch'an hsüan-chi*, vol. 1 (1956), pp. 262–79.

15. See the memorial essay to this sister written by Wu's friend Ch'eng T'ing-tso, in Ho Tse-han, p. 196; see also pp. 187–88.

16. Chin Chü's long poem is one of three written with identical rhymes and presented to Wu Ching-tzu on his thirtieth birthday (by Chinese count). The other two were written respectively by Wu Ch'ing and Chin Liang-ming, also Wu Ching-tzu's cousins. All three poems are reprinted in Ho Tse-han, pp. 164–71. See Chin Liang-ming's poem (Ho Tse-han, p. 169), which contains the lines: "Even as a young child, you were unlike other children,/Pulling books from the bookcase while yet a lisping boy."

17. For a list and a concise description of the Chinese classics, see Reischauer and Fairbank, pp. 64–68.

18. Because Wu Ch'ing's poem (Ho Tse-han, p. 164) mentions that Wu Ching-tzu was traveling about the Chiang-Huai area with his father at the age of seventeen (eighteen *sui*), some scholars have written that Wu began accompanying has father only at that age. But Wu himself, in a poem addressed to another cousin, the monk Hung-ming (*Wen-mu shan-fang chi*, 3/7a), says that "When I was fourteen [*sui*], I followed my father to his post/A thousand *li* to the ocean."

19. See Wu Ch'ing's poem in Ho Tse-han, p. 164. See Paul Stanley Ropp, "Early Ch'ing Society and Its Critics: The Life and Times of Wu Ching-tzu (1701–1754)" (Ph.D. diss., University of Michigan, 1974), p. 7.

20. Ho Tse-han, p. 170.

21. "Wen-mu hsien-sheng chuan," in ibid., pp. 182–84.

22. The terms quoted are taken from Wu Ch'ing's poem (Ho Tse-han, p. 165). For other accounts, see Chin Chü's poem (ibid., p. 167) and Chin Liang-ming's poem (ibid., p. 170). For Wu Ching-tzu's own descriptions of this period of his life, see the "Yi-chia *fu*", in *Wen-mu shan-fang chi*, 1/8a. See H. C. Chang's fine biography of Wu in his *Chinese Literature: Popular Fiction and Drama*, pp. 330–31.

23. See Wu Ching-tzu's second lyric to the tune "Mu-lan hua" (abbreviated form) in *Wen-mu shan-fang chi*, 4/2b. See in the same collection his lyric to the tune "Mai p'i-t'ang," 4/4ab, written in 1733.

24. Ho Tse-han, p. 165; see H. C. Chang, p. 331; and Ropp, p. 10.

25. *Wen-mu shan-fang chi*, 4/2b.

26. It had only been a little over eight years since Wu Lin-ch'i died in 1723; here, Wu is obviously practicing a bit of poetic license as well as exercising the Chinese habit of being imprecise with numbers.

27. See Ho Tse-han, pp. 199–20.

28. *Wen-mu shan-fang chi*, 4/3a.

29. These examinations were called *sui-shih* ("annual examinations") and

k'o-shih ("preliminary examinations"); passing the latter would qualify the student to proceed to the provincial examination which conferred the *chü-jen* degree and could thus open the door to high official appointment. Ropp, pp. 8–9, gives a good summary of the system.

30. Juan Chi (210–263) and Hsi K'ang (223–262) were recluses famous for their unconventionality and their fine poetry.

31. *Wen-mu shan-fang chi*, 4/4b. See Ropp, p. 13, for a different translation of this poem.

32. This guilt is expressed in various poems written after 1733. See, for example, his lyric to "Ju-yen fei," written on January 23, 1735, in *Wen-mu shan-fang chi*, 4/6b–7a. Ropp, p. 14, gives a complete translation of this lyric.

33. This wife's maiden name was Yeh, and she was the daughter of a Ch'üan-chiao physician. It is not really known whether she was the mother of all three of Wu Ching-tzu's younger sons; we only know that Wu's eldest son Lang was by his first wife. See Ho Tse-han, pp. 199–200 and section X of this chapter.

34. Chin Ho, who wrote the oft-quoted "postscript" *(pa)* to the 1869 Su-chou edition of the *Ju-lin wai-shih*, was also a distant relative of Wu Ching-tzu. See Ho Tse-han, p. 203.

35. Ch'en Ju-heng, "Wu Ching-tzu tsai Yang-chou" ("Wu Ching-tzu in Yang-chou"), *Wen-hsüeh yi-ch'an tseng-k'an*, vol. 8 (Peking, 1961), pp. 193–201.

36. I am here following the translation given by H. C. Chang, p. 338.

37. Ropp, pp. 16–17, 52, n. 49, gives an excellent account of the particulars of this examination.

38. *Wen-mu shan-fang chi*, hsü (prefaces) section, la.

39. See, for example, Wu Hsiao-ju, "Wu Ching-tzu chi ch'i *Ju-lin wai-shih*" ("Wu Ching-tzu and his *Ju-lih wai-shih*") in *Ju-lin wai-shih yen chiu lün-chi*, pp. 112–13; see Hu Shih, "Wu Ching-tzu nien-p'u," pp. 20–23.

40. Wu here uses a phrase, "ts'ai-hsing yu" ("the concern for gathering firewood"), which has its *locus classicus* in both the *Book of Rites (Li Chi)* and the *Mencius (Meng-tzu)*; the phrase is usually taken to be an euphemism for illness which prevents one from obeying a ruler's summons. Whether Wu Ching-tzu uses it here to refer to an actual illness (as used in the *Li Chi*) or to feigned illness (as used in the *Mencius*) is a debatable point. See Wu Hsiao-ju's discussion, ibid.

41. *Wen-mu shan-fang chi*, 2/9b–10a. In writing these lines, Wu was likely thinking of the eighth and last poem of the series entitled "Yung-shih shih" ("Poems on History") by the Six Dynasties poet Tso Ssu (250?–305?). In that poem, Tso also invokes the image of the caged bird to describe the frustrations of the luckless scholar, and concludes, as Wu seems to here, in a mood of resignation to the life of obscure self-cultivation.

42. The *Ch'üan-chiao hsien-chih*, 10/47ab, records that the temple sacrifices were to T'ai-po and *five hundred* worthies who came after him;

Chin Ho's postscript (in Ho Tse-han, p. 203) claims only "over two hundred and thirty."

43. Ho Tse-han devotes the entire first half of his book to the study of the actual persons and events fictionalized in the *Ju-lin wai-shih*.

44. "Hsin fa-hsien ti Wu Ching-tzu ti Chin-ling ching-wu t'u shih" ("Newly Discovered Poems of Wu Ching-tzu to Scenic Illustrations of Nanking"), in *Wen-hsüeh yen-chiu chi-k'an* (*Collection of Researches into Literature*), vol. 4 (Peking, 1956), pp. 277–78. See also the following article (pp. 288–93) by Fan Ning, "Kuan-yü Wu Ching-tzu ti 'Chin-ling ching-wu t'u shih' " ("Concerning Wu Ching-tzu's 'Poems to Scenic Illustrations of Nanking' ").

45. It is not impossible that Wu Ching-tzu might be referring to another sacrificial ceremony here and that there originally *were* sacrifices to T'ai-po. But that is highly unlikely.

46. T'ai-po is the subject of one section of the Confucian canon, the *Lun-yü* or *Analects*. See *A Concordance to the Analects of Confucius*, Harvard-Yenching Sinological Index Series, supplement 16, p. 14, sec. 8, no. 1. For a translation and an explanatory note, see Arthur Waley, trans., *The Analects of Confucius* (London, 1938), p. 132.

47. From Wang's long poem with preface which was written as an appendix to the poetry portion of the twelve *chüan Wen-mu shang-fang chi;* reprinted in Ho Tse-han, pp. 186–87. Hu Shih was aware of the existence of this poem, but apparently did not actually see it since he failed to take into account the important information in its preface concerning the date of Wu Ching-tzu's death.

48. Yüeh Heng-chün, "Shih-chi ti p'iao-po che—lün *Ju-lin wai'shih* ch'ün-hsiang" ("The Drifters of the Century—A Discussion of the *Ju-lin wai-shih's* Characters"), in *Hsien-tai wen-hsüeh* (*Contemporary Literature*), 45 (1971), 123–35, contains a good discussion of this point.

49. For Chin Chao-yen's relationship to Wu Ching-tzu, see Chang Hui-chien, "Wu Ching-tzu chiao-yu k'ao," pp. 360–61, and Ch'en Ju-heng, "Wu Ching-tzu tsai Yang-chou," p. 195. Chin Chao-yen was the son of Wu Ching-tzu's first cousin Chin Chü (see Ho Tse-han, pp. 166–169), who was also married to a sister of Wu's first wife (née T'ao). Chao-yen's son Chin T'ai-chün eventually married Wu's granddaughter. Although one generation below Wu, Chin Chao-yen was apparently on equal and friendly terms with him, and they traveled together frequently. See Ho Tse-han, pp. 102–14. Chin Chao-yen also wrote at least two extant poems concerning Wu Ching-tzu (see Ho Tse-han, pp. 188–89, 192–93), one of which is partially translated in section VIII of this chapter.

50. See Ho Tse-han, pp. 182–84. All subsequent references to Ch'eng Chin-fang's biography of Wu Ching-tzu will be taken from these pages.

51. See Chin Ho's postscript, reprinted in Ho Tse-han, p. 203, and the *Ch'üan-chiao hsien-chih*, 10/47ab.

52. Chang Hui-chien, "Wu Ching-tzu chiao-yu k'ao," p. 355, in which

Chang quotes a poem by Wu's friend Chou Chü. The question of Wu's residence or residences in Nanking is still not settled, but Meng Hsing-jen, in a newspaper story, claims to have located the site of Wu's principle Nanking dwelling by interviewing some of his descendants. See "Kuan-yü Wu Ching-tzu hsien-sheng ti yi-hsieh k'ou-ch'uan ts'ai-liao" ("Some Oral Material Concerning Mr. Wu Ching-tzu"), *Kuang-ming jih-pao* (*Kuang-ming Daily*), January 16, 1955, p. 3.

53. Hu Shih was not able to discover who this "Li-shan" was, but recently he is speculated to be Ch'eng Chin-ch'un (b. 1674), who was the brother of Wu Lin-ch'i's (Wu Ching-tzu's father's) minor wife. See Wang Wei-lin, pp. 170–72.

54. Chin Ho, in Ho Tse-han, p. 203.

55. See, for example, Senuma Saburō, "Jurin gaishi to sono chosha" ("The *Ju-lin wai-shih* and Its Author"), *Manmō* 16, no. 5 (May 1, 1935), 84; Tsukamoto Terukaya, "Go Kei-shi no Shōsetsu 'Jurin gaishi' ni tsuite" ("Concerning Wu Ching-tzu's Novel *Ju-lin wai-shih*"), Tōyō gaku (Tōhoku Daigaku), 1 (May, 1959), 47. For a more recent example, see the remarks concerning Wu Ching-tzu and the *Ju-lin wai-shih* in Chu-tsing Li, "Problems Concerning the Life of Wang Mien, Painter of Plum Blossoms," *Renditions* 6 (Spring, 1976), 119–20.

56. Reprinted in Ho Tse-han, pp. 180–82; this version, however, differs from the version reproduced in the original article reporting its discovery in several important places. See Ch'en Ju-heng, "Wu Ching-tzu *Wen-mu shan-fang chi* wai yi-wen ti fa-hsien," pp. 210–13. My opinion is that the reprint version makes more sense and is more reliable, since it is taken directly from Chiang Yü's extant work rather than copied from the second-hand version which came to the attention of its discoverer.

57. Fu-hsi is a legendary sage-king of ancient China, revered by Confucius as a high ancestor of the Chinese people.

58. Reprinted in Ho Tse-han, pp. 188–89.

59. Writes Ch'eng Chin-fang (Ho Tse-han, p. 189): "Even though his son secured an official post,/His poverty worsened from this time."

60. Ch'eng Chin-fang gives the date as "another seven days" after their last meeting on November 20, 1754. But no one accepts Ch'eng's account since Chin Chao-yen (see Ho Tse-han, pp. 192–93), who was called to Wu's deathbed, records it as "the evening before the last day of the moon in the first month of winter" or December 12 (the twenty-ninth day of the tenth month, by the lunar calendar). This is the date Hu Shih accepts. But Chin was writing in verse, and so might have sacrificed accuracy to the requirements of prosody. Wang Yu-tseng, who was also with Wu on that fatal day, sounds very certain about the date he gives in the prose preface to his poem about Wu Ching-tzu (Ho Tse-han, p. 186); I have thus followed Ho Tse-han in accepting his account.

61. The quatrain quoted is entitled "Tsung-yu Huai-nan" ("Carefree

Travel in Huai-nan") and is included in the *Ch'üan T'ang shih (Complete Collection of T'ang Dynasty Poems)* (Peking, n.d.), vol. 8, 501/5846. The complete poem is as follows: "A street of ten *li* links marketplaces/Where one gazes on immortals from a moonlit bridge./A man is born to die fittingly only in Yang-chou,/For the Ch'an Wisdom and Mountain View temples there make good cemeteries."

I am indebted to Professor L. S. Yang of Harvard University for identifying the actual author of these lines. See Ch'eng Chin-fang's poem "K'u Wu Min-hsüan" ("Grieving for Wu Min-hsüan"), in Ho Tse-han, p. 191, which includes the line: "In dying he was attracted to the good cemeteries of Yang-chou."

62. In the extant poetry of Wu's young friend Yen Ch'ang-ming are poems to recluses (*yin-yi*) whose lives are recorded in the *Nan Shih (History of the Southern Dynasty* [420–589]). These poems were written at a poetry session of young scholars at Wu Ching-tzu's house. See Hu Shih, "Wu Ching-tzu nien-p'u," p. 346.

63. Perhaps the only positive specimen of Wu's calligraphy still extant is that affixed to a painting depicting Lu Chien-tseng. See Chiao-jen, "Wu Ching-tzu shou-chi ti fa-hsien" ("The Discovery of the Handwriting of Wu Ching-tzu"), *Kuang-ming jih-pao*, December 1, 1957, p. 5. For Lu's biography, see Arthur W. Hummel, ed., *Eminent Chinese of the Ch'ing Period*, pp. 541–42.

64. See Chin Ho's postscript, in Ho Tse-han, p. 203.

65. Ho Tse-han (p. 173, 199) has determined that this first wife's maiden name was T'ao.

66. Ho Tse-han, pp. 199–200.

67. There are three poems by Wu Ching-tzu concerning him which evince a great deal of affection and fatherly concern in the *Wen-mu shan-fang chi* 3/5b and 3/12a.

68. Ch'eng Chin-fang in Ho Tse-han, p. 183. H. C. Chang, p. 340, n. 4, states without giving his source that Wu Lang became a *chin-shih* in 1754, "the year of his father's death."

69. Two small collections of his poems are appended to the four *chüan* edition of the *Wen-mu shan-fang chi*. There also exists a manuscript copy of a work entitled *Shan-t'ing chi (Collection of Mr. Fir Pavilion)*, with eleven *chüan* of poetry (*shih*) and five of lyrics (*tz'u*), preserved in the Chung-kuo k'o-shüeh yüan wen-hsüeh yen-chiu so (Literary Research Institute of the Chinese Academy of Sciences) in Peking. See Wang Wei-lin, pp. 172–75.

70. Wang, ibid.

71. See especially Chow Tse-tsung, *The May fourth Movement: Intellectual Revolution in Modern China* (Stanford, 1967), Chap. 11, for an authoritative summary of this movement.

72. One of the prose prefaces is the "Shang-shu ssu-hsüeh hsü" ("Preface to the Private Study of the *Book of History*"), written in "essay" (*san-wen)*

style and already cited earlier (see n. 56 above). The other is a piece of "parallel prose" (*p'ien-wen*), dated "three days before the double ninth in the twelfth year of Yung-cheng," or September 24, 1734, and written for a collection of poetry by Hsü Tzu-chih entitled "Yu-ch'ao shih-ts'ao" ("Poetic Grass for the Nest of Jade"). This text is also reproduced in its entirety in the article reporting its discovery; see Pien Hsiao-hsüan, "Fa-hsien yi-p'ien Wu Ching-tzu ti p'ien-wen" ("Discovering a Piece of Parallel Prose by Wu Ching-tzu"), *Kuang-ming jih-pao*, August 6, 1961, p. 4.

For information on recently discovered poems, calligraphy, and seals of Wu Ching-tzu, see n. 44 above; Chu Wan, "Wu Ching-tzu chi-wai shih yu yi-shou" ("Another Wu Ching-tzu Poem Not Included in His Collection"), *Kuang-ming jih-pao*, November 12, 1961, p. 4; "Wu Ching-tzu ti shih-kao cheng-li fa-piao" ("A Report on Putting in Order Drafts of Wu Ching-tzu's Poetry"), *Kuang-ming jih-pao*, December 12, 1956, p. 2; Ho Tse-han, p. 179.

73. Ho Tse-han, p. 204.

74. Reprinted in Ho Tse-han, pp. 178, 186–87.

75. Chin Ho, in Ho Tse-han, p. 204.

76. Ho Tse-han, pp. 176–77. See Wu Ch'ing's poem (Ho Tse-han, pp. 164–66) which, in describing Wu Ching-tzu's education, says he "Ventured into all the classics and history books."

77. See C. T. Hsia, *The Classic Chinese Novel*, p. 210, for a discussion of Wu Ching-tzu's views of the history of the Ming dynasty as seen in the *Ju-lin wai-shih*.

78. "Technique as Discovery," in *Approaches to the Novel*, ed. Robert Scholes (San Francisco, 1961), pp. 249–68.

Chapter Two

1. Included in *Essays of John Dryden*, ed. W. P. Ker (Oxford, 1900), II, 15–114.

2. *The Plot of Satire*, p. 6; hereafter cited as Kernan.

3. *Anatomy of Criticism*, p. 224; hereafter cited as Frye. Cited in Kernan, p. 13.

4. *A Brief History of Chinese Fiction*, pp. 288–89.

5. Frye, p. 154. The incident concerned may be found in Charles Lutwidge Dodgson, *The Complete Works of Lewis Carroll* (New York, 1936), pp. 233–50.

6. Similar distinctions between satire and pure humor are made in a number of studies. See, for example, Kernan, pp. 199–200, in which pure humor, which he calls by the more general name of "comedy," is described as different from satire because it is "thoughtless" and accepts "one's own nature and the world without undue puzzling over complex moral problems or trying to understand fully the mystery of life and nature." Satire, in contrast, "is intensely, persistently rational in its approach to life. . . . Its

consistent, unconcealed use of rhetoric, its overt contriving of effects, its regular use of . . . mock epic or beast fable establish the presence . . . of a shrewd, icy mind, carefully calculating poetic strategy, selecting details, and manipulating materials for a desired end." See also Ronald Paulson, *The Fictions of Satire* (Baltimore, 1967), p. 4; Leonard Feinberg, pp. 177–78; and Gilbert Highet, *The Anatomy of Satire*, pp. 154–55.

7. Quotations from the text of the *Ju-lin wai-shih* throughout this study are based on the English translation of Yang Hsien-yi and Gladys Yang, entitled *The Scholars* (Peking: Foreign Languages Press, 1957). I will deviate from this fine translation only when I feel that my own reading of the original text is either more accurate or can better illustrate whatever point I shall be making. This translation will hereafter be cited as *Scholars*. An American reprint (New York: Grosset and Dunlap, 1972) removed without explanation the original forward by the Chinese scholar Wu Tsu-hsiang and replaced it with one by the American critic C. T. Hsia. This change set back the original pagination by thirty pages.

In 1973, H. C. Chang of England translated chapters 31 and 32 of the novel, entitling them "Young Master Bountiful" and including them, along with a well-written introduction, in his book *Chinese Literature: Popular Fiction and Drama* (Edinburgh, 1973).

In 1975, the Jen-min wen-hsüeh ch'u-pan she of Peking did the scholarly world an immense service by producing a photographic copy of the 1803 Wo-hsien ts'ao-t'ang (Thatched Hall of Leisurely Repose) edition of the *Ju-lin wai-shih*, the oldest extant edition of the novel. This edition, which includes the commentary of an anonymous Chinese critic after each chapter, is the most authoritative text for scholarly study. But the reproduction fails to add consecutive pagination, making citation ambiguous and difficult. I have therefore used a modern edition published in August, 1969, by the T'ai-p'ing Book Co. in Hong Kong. This is one of several editions available which have been reproduced directly (with identical pagination) from the September, 1954, Tso-chia ch'u-pan she edition, one based faithfully on the 1803 original (except for chap. 56, which is deleted). This edition is cited below as *Ju-lin wai-shih*. The quotation can be found in *Ju-lin wai-shih*, pp. 108–9; *Scholars*, p. 169.

8. Ho Tse-han, pp. 143–44.

9. See Highet, pp. 155–56.

10. *Ju-lin wai-shih*, pp. 433–34; *Scholars*, pp. 583–84.

11. *The Power of Satire: Magic, Ritual, Art* (Princeton, 1960).

12. Elliott's contribution to the study of satire is nicely summarized in Kernan, pp. 9–12.

13. For example, Highet (pp. 151–54) regards them as the same thing.

14. *Essays of John Dryden*, II, 52.

15. Ibid., p. 79.

16. Ibid., p. 22.

17. Ibid., p. 100.

18. From "Verses on the Death of Dr. Swift," lines 459–60; quoted in Kernan, p. 14.

19. Highet, p. 16.

20. Kernan, pp. 21–22, has written that "Satirists do locate the causes of corruption in different persons and institutions, but the differences are only nominal. . . . Swift understood that . . . the objects of satire . . . are strangely limited in number and kind, and the history of satire bears him out. However various the accents spoken by the men and women who inhabit satire, however different the clothing they wear, the streets they walk, and the cities they dirty, they exert the same kind of pressure on society and nature, and create the same kind of world."

21. Highet, pp. 148–230.

22. Feinberg, p. 128.

23. Quoted in Highet, p. 148.

24. Quoted in Elliott, p. 242.

25. See Kernan, p. 5.

26. "T'an feng-tz'u" ("Discussing Satire"), Wen-yi pao (Bulletin of Literary Art), no. 160 (July 30, 1956), p 17.

27. Kernan, pp. 25–26.

28. Theory of Literature, 3d ed. (New York, 1956), p. 35.

29. See James J. Y. Liu, Chinese Theories of Literature (Chicago, 1975), pp. 106–16. See also James J. Y. Liu, The Art of Chinese Poetry (Chicago, 1962), pp. 65–69, 92.

30. See Kuo Shao-yü, Chung-kuo wen-hsüeh p'i-p'ing shih (History of Chinese Literary Criticism), rev. ed., (Hong Kong, n.d.), pp. 37–40. The "Tien-lun lun-wen," originally included in chüan 52 of the sixth-century Wen-hsüan (Literary Anthology) of Hsiao T'ung (501–531), has been reprinted in a number of places. My source: Pei-ching ta-hsüeh Chung-kuo wen-hsüeh shih chiao-yen shih (Teaching and research office for the history of Chinese literature, Peking University), ed., Wei-Chin Nan-pei ch'ao wen-hsüeh shih ts'an-k'ao tzu-liao (Reference Material for the Literary History of the Six Dynasties), (Hong Kong, n.d.), pp. 45–52.

31. Translation is by the late Ch'en Shih-hsiang, reprinted under the title "Essay on Literature" in Cyril Birch, ed., Anthology of Chinese Literature: From Early Times to the Fourteenth Century (New York, 1965), p. 214. The original text of the Wen-fu can be found in chüan 17 of Hsiao T'ung's Wen-hsüan. Other English translations are by E. R. Hughes, The Art of Letters, Lu Chi's "Wen Fu," A.D. 302 (New York, 1951), and Achilles Fang, "Rhymeprose on Literature: The Wen-fu of Lu Chi (A.D. 261–303)," Harvard Journal of Asiatic Studies 14 (1951), 527–66.

32. First chapter, entitled "Yüan-tao" ("Tracing the Origin of the Tao"), in Wen-hsin tiao-lung chu (Annotated Edition of The Literary Mind: Elab-

orations), vol. 1 *chüan* 1, annotated by Fan Wen-lan (Peking; 1958), pp. 1–3; hereafter cited as *Wen-hsin*. My translation largely follows that of Vincent Shih, *The Literary Mind and the Carving of Dragons* (New York, 1950), p. 12, hereafter cited as *Literary Mind*. Unless otherwise noted, all other quotations of the *Wen-hsin* in this study will be based on Shih's translation.

33. The second chapter of the *Wen-hsin* is therefore called "Cheng-sheng" or "Evidence from the Sage"; this is followed by "Tsung-ching" or "Classics as Literary Sources." See *Wen-hsin*, pp. 15–23; *Literary Mind*, pp. 13–21.

34. See the definition offered by Edward Schafer in his *First Supplement to Matthews* (Berkeley, 1973), p. 25, no. 401.

35. "Notes on the Wind: The Term 'Feng' in Chinese Literary Criticism," in *Transition and Permanence: Chinese History and Culture*, pp. 285–93.

36. Translation of this and the subsequent quotation from the *Major Preface* is by Gibbs, ibid., pp. 288, 293; my italics. Brackets substituted for parentheses in the original. See the translation of James J. Y. Liu, *Chinese Theories of Literature*, p. 112.

37. See, for example, Vincent Shih's rendering of *chüan* 9 of *Wen-hsin* (p. 157) in *Literary Mind*, p. 50; or Teng Ssu-yü's translation of the sixth-century *Yen-shih chia-hsün*, ed. Chou Fa-kao (Taipei, 1960), 2/4a, 9/56a. The translation is entitled *Family Instructions for the Yen Clan* (Leiden, 1968); pp. 5 and 91 correspond respectively to the Chinese text cited.

38. *Wen-hsin*, I, 270; *Literary Mind*, pp. 78–79.

39. *Wen-hsin*, I, 272; *Literary Mind*, p. 83; my translation here differs greatly from Shih's.

40. *Essays of John Dryden*, II, 80.

41. *Ju-lin wai-shih*, pp. 45-46; *Scholars*, pp. 88–89.

42. Liu Chi's biography is in the *Ming Shih (Ming History)*, *chüan* 128 (K'ai-ming Bookstore *Er-shih-wu shih* edition [1934], IX, 313–14).

43. Chao P'u's biography is in the *Sung Shih (Sung History)*, *chüan* 256 (K'ai-ming Bookstore *Er-shih-wu shih* edition [1934], VI, 708–9).

44. *The Rise of the Novel* (Berkeley, 1957), p. 13.

45. Frye, p. 303. See R. C. Elliott, who writes: "Is *Gulliver* a novel? Probably not, although it is not easy to say (except by arbitrary stipulation) why it is not. Clearly it is satire. . . . Arthur E. Case . . . thinks that . . . 'it would be more accurate and more illuminating to call it a politico-sociological treatise much of which is couched in the medium of satire' " (*The Power of Satire*, pp. 184–185).

46. Frye, p. 309.

47. Elliott, pp. 187–88.

Chapter Three

1. See *The Cankered Muse* (New Haven, 1959), pp. 1–7. Also see chap. 2, n. 20 above.

2. The Japanese scholar Ogawa Tamaki was the first to note the similarity of structure between the *Water Margin* and the *Ju-lin wai-shih*; see "Jurin Gaishi no keishiki to naiyō," in his *Chūgoku shōsetsu-shi no kenkyū* pp. 184–86. See Ho Man-tzu, *Lün Ju-lin wai-shih*, pp. 75–77. Hsia's assertion is explained in *The Classic Chinese Novel*, pp. 207–8.

3. The term "nihilist" is applied specifically to those who find no positive moral value or standard in the *Ju-lin wai-shih*. It does not imply that they themselves have no moral values whatsoever, or even that they hold to no moral values vis-à-vis literature as a whole.

4. The text of this brief speech is reprinted in *Wen-hsüeh yi-ch'an hsüan-chi*, vol. 1 (Peking, 1956), pp. 239–41.

5. This speech has been translated into many languages. See *Mao Tse-tung on Literature and Art*, 3d ed., (Peking, 1967), p. 30.

6. For a good summary of the Marxist view of "realism," its connection with historical progress, and its relevance to Wu Ching-tzu's world view, see Su Hung-ch'ang, "Kuan-yü Wu Ching-tzu ti shih-chieh-kuan ho ch'uang-tso fang-fa" ("Concerning the World View and the Creative Methods of Wu Ching-tzu"), in *Ming-Ch'ing hsiao-shuo yen-chiu lün-wen chi*, pp. 283–85.

7. *Lün Ju-lin wai-shih*, p. 17. Ho, however, was later attacked as a "rightist" for allegedly equating Wu Ching-tzu's attack on the Ch'ing "ruling class" with an attack on *all* ruling classes, including China's Communist rulers. See Yang Huai, "Yu-p'ai fen-tzu Ho Man-tzu hsieh ti 'Lün Ju-lin wai-shih' shih-yi-pu fan-tung tso-p'in" ("The Discussing the 'Ju-lin wai-shih' Written by the Rightist Ho Man-tzu is a Reactionary Work"), *Kuang-ming jih-pao*, December 8, 1957, p. 5.

8. "*Ju-lin wai-shih* ti ssu-hsiang ho yi-shu" ("The Thought and Artistry of the *Ju-lin wai-shih*"), in *Ju-lin wai-shih yen-chiu lün-chi*, p. 6.

9. "Wu Ching-tzu ho t'a-ti shih-tai" (cited in chap. 1, n. 14), pp. 276–77.

10. "Wu Ching-tzu ti hsiao-shuo *Ju-lin wai-shih*" ("Wu Ching-tzu's Novel *Ju-lin wai-shih*"), *Wen-hsüeh yen-chiu chi-k'an*, vol. 1 (Peking, 1955), p. 16.

11. "Wu C   _-tzu Chi-ch'i *Ju-lin wai-shih*" (cited in chap. 1, n. 39), p. 123.

12. "Jurin Gaishi no keishiki to naiyō," p. 189.

13. Ibid., pp. 191–92.

14. The translation was published by Heibonsha (Tokyo, 1962) as vol. 23 of the *Chūgoku koten bungaku zenshū (Collection of Classical Chinese literature)*.

15. "Jurin Gaishi no iwayuru kōteiteki jimbutsu ni tsuite," in *Tōkyō Gakugei Daigaku kenkyū hōkoku* 13, no. 11 (1962), 23.
16. Ibid., p. 24.
17. Ibid., pp. 24–25.
18. Ibid., p. 26.
19. Ibid., p. 27.
20. Ibid., pp. 27–28.
21. "Shih-chi ti p'iao-po-che–lün Ju-lin wai-shih ti ch'ün-hsiang" (cited in chap. 1, 48), 134.
22. Inada, p. 28; Yüeh, p. 135.
23. "Protest Against Conventions and Conventions of Protest," in Arthur F. Wright, ed., *Confucianism and Chinese Civilization*, pp. 231–32.
24. Ibid., p. 250.
25. See "The Amateur Ideal in Ming and Early Ch'ing Society: Evidence from Painting," in Joseph R. Levenson, *Confucian China and Its Modern Fate: A Trilogy*, pp. 15–43.
26. "Confucian Eremitism in the Yüan Period," in Arthur F. Wright, ed., *Confucianism and Chinese Civilization*, p. 256.
27. The opening chapter, which contains the story of Wang Mien, bears this explanatory title: "In giving the prologue, [this chapter] briefly presents the overall meaning;/Through a famous man, it indirectly covers the entire work." Likewise, Chapter 55, which gives the account of the four eccentrics, begins with the title: "Adding four characters [this chapter] recounts the past and provides thought for the future. . . ." In both cases, the idea of a thematic summary is clear.
28. While the four eccentrics are, in all likelihood, purely fictional, the character Wang Mien is patterned after an historical personage. See Chu-tsing Li, "Problems Concerning the Life of Wang Mien, Painter of Plum Blossoms" (cited in chap. 1, n. 55), for an excellent summary of the various accounts of Wang in Chinese history.
29. *Ju-lin wai-shih*, p. 1; *Scholars*, pp. 33–34.
30. *Ju-lin wai-shih*, p. 522; *Scholars*, p. 706.
31. "Confucian Eremitism in the Yüan Period," p. 256.
32. Ibid., pp. 254–55.
33. *Ju-lin wai-shih*, pp. 2–3; *Scholars*, pp. 35–36.
34. *Ju-lin wai-shih*, pp. 5–6; *Scholars*, p. 40.
35. See *A Concordance to Meng Tzu*, Harvard-Yenching Sinological Index Series, Supplement 17, p. 24, sec. 3B, no. 7. See also D. C. Lau, trans., *Mencius* (Middlesex, England, 1970), p. 112.
36. Tuan-kan Mu is remembered as just such a "worthy" by Ssu-ma Ch'ien in his *Records of the Grand Historian*. See *Shih-chi, chüan* 44 (K'ai-ming Bookstore *Er-shih-wu shih* ed. [1934], I, 155).
37. *Ju-lin wai-shih*, p. 4; *Scholars*, p. 37.
38. *Ju-lin wai-shih*, p. 11; *Scholars*, p. 48.

39. "Confucian Eremitism in the Yüan Period," pp. 254–55.
40. *Ju-lin wai-shih*, pp. 532–33; *Scholars*, p. 707.
41. *Ju-lin wai-shih*, pp. 535–38; *Scholars*, 710–14.
42. *Ju-lin wai-shih*, pp. 538–39; *Scholars*, p. 714.
43. *Ju-lin wai-shih*, p. 535; *Scholars*, p. 710.
44. *A Concordance to Meng Tzu*, p. 14, sec. 2B, no. 2; Lau, *Mencius*, p. 87. See Mote, p. 269.
45. *A Concordance to Meng Tzu*, p. 41, sec. 5B, no. 7; Lau, *Mencius*, p. 157.
46. *Ju-lin wai-shih*, pp. 9–10; *Scholars*, pp. 45–46.
47. See the "preface" *(hsü)*, pp. 2b–3a, in the 1975 reprint of the 1803 Wo-hsien ts'ao-t'ang edition of the *Ju-lin wai-shih* (Peking: Jen-min wen-hsüeh ch'u-pan she). See, in the same edition, the remarks of an anoymous commentator (1/19b–20a): "The four graphs *kung-ming fu-kuei* are the primary key to the whole book. That is why they are mentioned at the very start. Though they are only slightly touched upon here, hereafter [we see that], of the myriad changes and permutations [of plot], nothing occurs but which emanates from these graphs."
48. *Ju-lin wai-shih*, p. 157; *Scholars*, p. 233.
49. "Protest Against Conventions and Conventions of Protest," pp. 227–31.
50. Perhaps because of its graphic descriptions of unpleasant bodily functions, this scene is not included in *The Scholars*. I quote it here in my own translation because it clearly demonstrates Kuang's exemplary filial piety before his involvement with officialdom. See *Ju-lin wai-shih*, p. 161.
51. Deathbed scenes with similar exhortations to eremitic virtues include (1) Wang Mien's mother's (*Ju-lin wai-shih*, p. 9; *Scholars*, p. 44) and (2) Tu Shao-ching's faithful old family servant Mr. Lou's (*Ju-lin wai-shih*, pp. 322–23; *Scholars*, pp. 442–43).
52. *Ju-lin wai-shih*, p. 170; *Scholars*, p. 251.
53. *Ju-lin wai-shih*, p. 201; *Scholars*, pp. 290–91.
54. *Ju-lin wai-shih*, p. 197; *Scholars*, p. 285.
55. See Ropp (cited in chap. 1, n. 19) for a thorough discussion of three of these themes: examinations, women, and superstition. See Timothy C. Wong, "Satire and the Polemics of the Criticism of Chinese Fiction: A Study of the *Ju-lin wai-shih*" (Ph. D. diss., Stanford University, 1975), esp. pp. 161–234.
56. *A Concordance to the Analects of Confucius*, p. 14, sec. 8, no. 1. The translation is by Authur Waley, *The Analects of Confucius*, p. 132; see also n. 1 on the same page.
57. On this point, see Tu Wei-ming's illuminating article "*Li* [Ritual] as a Process of Humanization," *Philosophy East and West* 22, no. 2 (April, 1972), 187–200. "In the Confucian context," writes Tu, "it is inconceivable that one can become truly human without going through the process of

'ritualization,' which in this particular connection means humanization"
(p. 198).

58. For a recent discussion of this in English, see Paul S. Ropp, "The
Seeds of Change: Reflections on the Condition of Women in the Early and
Mid Ch'ing," *Signs: Journal of Women in Culture and Society* 2, no. 1
(Autumn, 1976), 11–13.

59. *Ju-lin wai-shih*, p. 337; *Scholars*, pp. 463–64. The poem concerned
has been rendered into English by James Legge as follows:

> 1. Says the wife, "It is cock-crow";
> Says the husband, "It is grey dawn."
> "Rise, Sir, and look at the night,
> If the morning star be not shining.
> Bestir yourself, and move about,
> To shoot the wild ducks and geese.
>
> 2. "When your arrows and line have found them,
> I will dress them fitly for you.
> When they are dressed, we will drink [together over them],
> And I will hope to grow old with you.
> Your lute in your hands
> Will emit its quiet pleasant tones.
>
> 3. "When I know those whose acquaintance you wish,
> I will give them of the ornaments of my girdle.
> When I know those with whom you are cordial,
> I will send to them of the ornaments of my girdle.
> When I know those whom you love,
> I will repay their friendship from the ornaments of my girdle."

See *The Chinese Classics*, vol. 4 (Hong Kong, 1960), pp. 134–36.

60. *Ju-lin wai-shih*, p. 406; *Scholars*, p. 551.
61. *Ju-lin wai-shih*, p. 438; *Scholars*, p. 590.

Chapter Four

1. See Kernan, pp. 17–18.
2. Ibid., pp. 95–104.
3. *The Classic Chinese Novel*, p. 6.
4. Included in Chiang Jui-ts'ao, *Hsiao-shuo k'ao-cheng hsü-p'ien shih-yi
(Supplement to Research Materials for Fiction)* (Taipei, 1971), p. 561.
5. *Hu Shih wen-ts'un*, vol. 2, *chüan* 2, p. 173.
6. *An introduction to Chinese Literature* (Bloomington, 1966), p. 246.
7. Kernan, pp. 96–100.
8. Ibid., pp. 100–101.
9. Ibid., pp. 81–91.

10. *Ju-lin wai-shih*, pp. 200–201; *Scholars*, p. 290.

11. *Ju-lin wai-shih*, p. 45; *Scholars*, pp. 87–88.

12. *Ju-lin wai-shih*, pp. 77–78; *Scholars*, pp. 129–30.

13. *Ju-lin wai-shih*, pp. 206–32; *Scholars*, pp. 296–328.

14. *Ju-lin wai-shih*, pp. 22–23; *Scholars*, pp. 60–61.

15. *Ju-lin wai-shih*, pp. 532; *Scholars*, p. 706. Li Po (701–762) and Tu Fu (712–770) are considered China's most illustrious poets; Tseng Shen and Yen Hui are disciples of Confucius and paragons of moral rectitude.

16. The sixteenth-century novel *Water Margin* is a good case in point. See Richard Gregg Irwin, *The Evolution of a Chinese Novel* (Cambridge, Mass., 1966) pp. 66–75.

17. See Wu Tsu-hsiang (cited in chap. 3, n. 8 above), p. 29; see Ch'eng Chih-t'ing, "Tu *Ju-lin wai-shih* sui-pi" ("Casual Jottings on Reading the *Ju-lin wai-shih*"), in *Wen-hsüeh tsa-chih (Literature Magazine)*, 3, no. 6 (1958), 12–16.

18. See discussion of pure invective and pure humor in chapter 2 above. See C. T. Hsia, pp. 206–8.

19. See chap. 3, n. 2, above.

20. See Irwin, p. 118. Irwin provides a convenient plot summary of the 120-chapter version; pp. 150–151 and the complete translation of chapter 120 on pp. 184–201 are relevant to our discussion.

21. *Ju-lin wai-shih*, p. 369; *Scholars*, p. 506.

22. *Ju-lin wai-shih*, p. 377; *Scholars*, p. 514.

23. H. C. Chang, *Chinese Literature: Popular Fiction and Drama*, p. 344, questions the authenticity of these chapters. See also n. 1 on the same page.

24. " 'Ju-lin wai-shih' ti ssu-hsiang ho yi-shu," pp. 31–33. The term *p'i-li yang-ch'iu* was originally *p'i-li ch'un-ch'iu* (or, literally, "[the technique of] subsurface criticism of the *Spring and Autumn Annals* [of Confucius]"). During the late fourth-century reign of the Chien-wen emperor of the Tsin dynasty, there was a taboo on the word *ch'un* and the phrase was changed to *p'i-li yang-ch'iu*. To a traditional Chinese the phrase immediately conjures up the classical Confucian technique of subtle censure.

25. *Ju-lin wai-shih*, pp. 16–17; *Scholars*, pp. 52–53.

26. See P. D. Hanan, "The Early Chinese Short Story: A Critical Theory in Outline," *Harvard Journal of Asiatic Studies* 27 (1967), esp. pp. 172–78.

27. There have been various studies of the *Ju-lin wai-shih*'s use of the vernacular from a linguistic point of view. These include a "New Preface" by Ch'ien Hsüan-t'ung, attached to two different editions of the *Ju-lin wai-shih* published by the Ya-tung t'u-shu kuan of Shanghai in 1920 and 1922; Hsü Chung-yü, "*Ju-lin wai-shih* ti yü-yen yi-shu" ("The Linguistic Art of the *Ju-lin wai-shih*"), *Yü-wen hsüeh-hsi (Language Study)*, 33 (May, 1955), 42–48; Kuei Ping-ch'üan, "Lüeh-t'an *Ju-lin wai-shih* ti jen-wu hsing-hsiang ho yü-wen wu-se" ("A Brief Discussion of the Characterization

and Linguistic Features of the *Ju-lin wai-shih*"), *Wen-hsüeh yi-ch'an tseng-k'an*, no. 1 (Peking, 1955), pp. 61–69; Kuei Ping-ch'uan, *"Ju-lin wai shih* ti fang-yen k'ou-yü" ("Regional Expressions of the *Ju-lin wai-shih*"), *Wen-hsüeh yi-ch'an tseng-k'an*, no. 5 (Peking, 1957), pp. 340–54. In addition, the Japanese linguist Kōsaka Junichi has recognized that the *Ju-lin wai-shih* is an important source for linguistic studies of colloquial Chinese in the Ch'ing period and published an index to what he considers the most important examples of vernacular phrases and grammatical usage. See *Jurin gaishi goi sakuin (Index to the Vocabulary of the* Ju-lin wai-shih) (Osaka, 1971).

28. See n. 26 above.

29. *Ju-lin wai-shih*, p. 400; *Scholars*, p. 543.

30. *Ju-lin wai-shih*, p. 30; *Scholars*, p. 69.

31. *Ju-lin wai-shih*, p. 23; all such formulaic commentary has been left out of *The Scholars*.

32. *Ju-lin wai-shih*, p. 17; *Scholars*, p. 53.

33. *Ju-lin wai-shih*, p. 87; *Scholars*, p. 143.

34. *The Power of Satire*, pp. 130–222. See also Kernan's summary of Elliott's arguments, *The Plot of Satire*, pp. 10–11.

35. What dreams there are are either nonsatirical (Wang Hui's in Chapter 2) or directed toward characterization. supporting, rather than making, the satirical point (Mei Chiu's dream in the same chapter). See the discussion in Chapter 5 below.

36. *Ju-lin wai-shih*, pp. 226–27; *Scholars*, p. 322.

37. See the discussion of this same speech in Wu Tsu-hsiang, pp. 36–37.

38. From the Hsing-yüan t'ui-shih Preface to the Ch'i-hsing T'ang (1874) edition of the *Jul-lin wai-shih*, reprinted in Ho Tse-han, p. 206.

39. The terms "showing" and "telling" are discussed by Wayne C. Booth in his *Rhetoric of Fiction* (Chicago, 1961), pp. 3–20.

Chapter Five

1. See Damian Grant, *Realism* (London, 1970), esp. pp. 1–19.

2. This has been a common tendency of many American critics. See, for example, John L. Bishop, "Some Limitations of Chinese Fiction," *Far Eastern Quarterly* 15 (1956), 239–47; or C. T. Hsia, *Classic Chinese Novel*, introduction, esp. p. 6.

3. W. L. Idema, *Chinese Vernacular Fiction: The Formative Period* (Leiden, 1974), pp. 50–56.

4. Idema explains (pp. 55–56) that, by pointing out the misleading effects of directly applying Western realism to early Chinese vernacular fiction, he is not implying "the impossibility of applying western concepts to Chinese literature" but is only saying that these concepts should not be applied without careful reflection.

5. *The Rise of the Novel*, pp. 9–34.

6. "On the 'Scientific' Study of Modern Chinese Literature: A Reply to Professor Prusek," *T'oung Pao* 50 (1963), 430.

7. The didactic or rhetorical concerns of satire are discussed in almost any extensive work on the subject. For a recent example, see John R. Clark and Anna Motto, *Satire: That Blasted Art* (New York, 1973), pp. 1–23.

8. "Several Artistic Methods in the Classic Chinese Novel *Ju-lin wai-shih*," *Archiv Orientalni* 32 (January, 1964), 22–23.

9. *The Classic Chinese Novel*, p. 242.

10. *Ju-lin wai-shih*, pp. 27–28; *Scholars*, pp. 65–66.

11. *Ju-lin wai-shih*, pp. 18–19; *Scholars*, pp. 55–56.

12. *Ju-lin wai-shih*, p. 159; *Scholars*, pp. 236–37.

13. *Ju-lin wai-shih*, p. 519; *Scholars*, pp. 690–91.

Chapter Six

1. See Bishop, p. 245; also C. T. Hsia, *The Classic Chinese Novel*, pp. 299–306.

2. Feng's collection, the first of three, is entitled *Ku-chin hsiao-shuo*, or *Stories Old and New*, and the stories referred to are, respectively, nos. 8 and 16. For an English translation of the Wu Pao-an story, see "The Journey of the Corpse" in Cyril Birch, trans., *Stories from a Ming Collection* (New York, 1958), pp. 129–49; for the story of Fan Chü-ch'ing, see John L. Bishop, trans., "Fan Chü-ch'ing's Eternal Friendship" in John L. Bishop, *The Colloquial Short Story in China* (Cambridge, Mass., 1965), pp. 88–99. On the *Chin P'ing Mei*, see P. D. Hanan, "A Landmark of the Chinese Novel," *University of Toronto Quarterly* 30, no. 3 (April, 1961), 325–35.

3. Andrew H. Plaks. *Archetype and Allegory in the "Dream of the Red Chamber"* (Princeton, 1976), p. 11.

4. See Lucien Miller, *Masks of Fiction in "Dream of the Red Chamber": Myth, Mimesis, and Persona* (Tucson, 1975), pp. 5–16.

5. The translation is by David Hawkes and taken from volume 1 of his projected five-volume complete translation of the *Red Chamber Dream*. See *The Story of the Stone* (Harmondsworth, England, 1973), pp. 20–21.

Appendix

1. See chap. 1, sec. VII, above.

2. See Sun K'ai-ti, *Chung-kuo t'ung-su hsiao-shuo shu-mu*, pp. 198–200; Iida Yoshirō, "Jurin gaishi no kenkyū to shiryō," in *Chūgoku no hachi dai shōsetsu*, pp. 309–12; Kawano Masaaki, "Jurin gaishi kō," *Kan bungaku* 11 (August, 1964), 19–25.

3. I have unfortunately not been able to secure a sixty-chapter version of the *Ju-lin wai-shih* and have to rely on the description of others. See Chao Ts'ung, "Ch'ung-yin *Ju-lin wai-shih* hsü" ("Preface to a New Printing of the *Ju-lin wai-shih*") in the 1963 edition of the *Ju-lin wai-shih* published

by Yu-lien ch'u-pan she in Hong Kong. See also H. C. Chang, pp. 341–42, esp. n. 1 and n. 2.

   4. See Chao Ts'ung, ibid.; Ho Tse-han, p. 180; and H. C. Chang, p. 342.

   5. *Chinese Popular Fiction in Two London Libraries*, p. 335. There is also speculation that this "busybody" is the same person who wrote the new preface, that is, Hsi-hung-sheng of Tungwu. See Sun K'ai-ti, p. 287, and Ho Tse-han, p. 180.

   6. *Chung-kuo t'ung-su hsiao-shuo shu-mu*, pp. 198–200.

   7. Reprinted in Ho Tse-han, p. 205.

   8. I have examined a copy of this rare book in the Tōyō Bunko in Tokyo. It was published in two *chüan* by Pao-wen ko (Precious Literature Alcove) in 1885 (the eleventh year of Kuang-hsü). *Chüan* 1 contains sixty-eight double pages, and includes a preface by Huang An-chin who claims the work includes commentary by his father Huang Hsiao-t'ien. *Chüan* 2 has fifty-nine double pages and an abridged version of Chin Ho's postscript. The entire work is credited to T'ien-mu shan ch'iao, a name which appears both on the title page and at the end of the second *chüan*. T'ien-mu shan ch'iao is the pen-name of Chang Wen-hu, and Sun K'ai-ti credits the authorship of this work to Chang in his *Catalogue*, p. 200. Hu Shih is apparently mistaken in listing this as two separate works in his chronological biography of Wu Ching-tzu (*Hu Shih wen-ts'un*, 2, 4/48). See also Liu Ts'un-yan, p. 335.

   9. 2/3a.

   10. *Chinese Popular Fiction in Two London Libraries*, p. 54.

   11. See chap. 4, sec. II, above.

   12. See Richard G. Irwin, pp. 118, 200. Irwin gives a complete English translation of the last chapter (120) in *Water Margin*, in which the Sung emperor, on the advice of Chamberlain Su, issues a decree conferring posthumous honors on Sung Chiang and all the bandit heroes of the Liang-shan lair.

   13. Quoted in Ho Man-tzu, p. 76. The "yu-pang" chapter from which the quotation comes can be found in many modern editions, including the two Ya-tung t'u-shu kuan editions listed above.

   14. See Ho Man-tzu, pp. 75–77.

   15. Ho Tse-han, p. 183. Kawano Masaaki, p. 20, reports on a fifty-chapter text supposedly published by the Chiang-su shu-chü in 1874, but says the text is no longer extant.

   16. Liu Ts'un-yan, p. 335, points out that *chüan* and *hui* may not necessarily be the same thing and hence fifty *chüan* may actually contain the fifty-five or more *hui* which make up the text of the *Ju-lin wai-shih*. But this seems unlikely since Chin Ho's postscript refers to the chapters of the *Ju-lin wai-shih* as *chüan*, including the Chapter 56 he wants deleted.

17. *Ch'üan-chiao hsien-chih, ts'e* 5, 10/47ab, contains Wu's biography; the reference to the *Ju-lin wai-shih* being in 50 *chüan* is found in the bibliography in *ts'e* 8, 15/5b.
18. Yeh's work is collected in the collectanea *Ts'ung-shu chi-ch'eng ch'u-pien*, no. 2967 (Shanghai, 1936). The reference to the *Ju-lin wai-shih* is on p. 2.
19. See Yang Chung-hsi's comments, reprinted in Ho Tse-han, p. 185; Hsü K'o, *Ch'ing pai-lei ch'ao (Notes on Ch'ing Dynasty Fiction)* (Shanghai, 1920), 67/40–41; Yü Yüeh's comments in K'ung Ling-ching, ed., *Chung-kuo hsiao-shuo shih-liao (Historical Materials on Chinese Fiction)* (Taipei, 1965), p. 143. Yü mentions that he is following Yeh Ming-feng.
20. *Hu Shih wen-ts'un;* vol. 2, chüan 4, p. 47.

Selected Bibliography

In listing Wu Ching-tzu's extant works below, I have tried to be comprehensive. But I am reluctant to cite texts I have not personally seen, and some of the collections in which Wu's poems appear have not been available to me, necessitating my dependence on reprints.

Secondary sources listed in this bibliography are limited to those books and articles deemed most pertinent and important to this study. Readers who have need of a more exhaustive bibliography on Wu Ching-tzu are advised to consult either my dissertation ("Satire and the Polemics of the Criticism of Chinese Fiction: A study of the *Ju-lin wai-shih,*" Stanford, 1975) or that of Paul Stanley Ropp cited below.

PRIMARY SOURCES

1. Poetry

Chin-ling ching-wu t'u shih (Verses to Illustrations of Nanking Scenes). Twenty-three poems discovered in Ch'ang-sha, the capital of Hunan province, in 1956 and rendered in various styles of calligraphy by Wu Ching-tzu's friend Fan Ming-cheng in 1753. Edited by Pei-ching ta-hsüeh wen-hsüeh yen-chiu so (Literary Research Institute of Peking University) and reprinted entirely in *Wen-hsüeh yen-chiu chi-k'an (Collection of Studies of Literature),* vol. 1 (Peking: Jen-min wen-hsüeh ch'u-pan she, 1956), pp. 272–87. Also included in the 1957 Ku-tien wen-hsüeh ch'u-pan she edition of the *Wen-mu shan-fang chi.*

"Chiang-shang tsu-feng yü Wang Che-t'ien Li Yü-men tso" ("Written with Wang Che-t'ien and Li Yü-men While Riding Against the Wind on the Yangtze"). A recently discovered poem reprinted in Chu Wan, "Wu Ching-tzu chi-wai shih yu yi-shou" ("Yet another Wu Ching-tzu Poem Outside His Collection"), "Wen-hsüeh y-ch'an" ("Literary Heritage"), *Kuang-ming jih-pao (Kuang-ming Daily),* 388 (November 12, 1961), p. 4.

"Hsi-hu kuei-chou yu-kan" ("Feelings on Returning to the Boat at West Lake"). One of three poems, not in the extant *Wen-mu shan-fang chi,* which Ogawa Tamaki cited in a 1947 article as written by Wu Ching-tzu. Subsequently, the other two have been shown actually to have

151

been written by Wu's son Wu Lang. This poem is also appended to the
Ku-tien edition of the *Wen-mu shan-fang chi,* under the title "Hsi-hu
kuei-chou tso" ("Written on Returning to the Boat at West Lake").
*Wen-mu shan-fang chi (Collection of the Mountain Retreat of Literary
Trees).* Secured by a Peking bookstore for Hu Shih in 1921. A collection of Wu Ching-tzu's poems in four *chüan,* plus two *chüan* of poetry
by Wu Lang and informative prefaces by seven of Wu Ching-tzu's
contemporaries. Subsequently, this important collection was published by the Ya-tung t'u-shu kuan of Shanghai in June, 1931, in an
edition which included a new preface by Hu Shih as well as Hu's
chronological biography of Wu Ching-tzu. In 1957, the Ku-tien wen-
hsüeh ch'u-pan she of Shanghai published a copy of the Ya-tung edition, deleting all of Hu Shih's material but adding the now available
Chin-ling ching-wu t'u shih.
Untitled poem. Reported in Chiao-jen, "Wu Ching-tzu shou-chi ti fa-
hsien" ("The Discovery of Wu Ching-tzu's Handwriting"), in "Wen-
hsüeh yi-ch'an," *Kuang-ming jih-pao* 185 (December 1, 1957), p. 5.
Written by Wu in 1740 and rendered in his own calligraphy on a
painting of his benefactor Lu Chien-tseng (1690–1768).

2. Prose
"Shang-shu ssu-hsüeh hsü" ("Preface to the *Private Study of the* Book of
History"). Reprinted in Ho Tse-han, pp. 180–82. Originally, this preface was attached to a study of a Confusian classic by Chiang Yü
(1706–1770). Its discovery was reported by Ch'en Ju-heng in "Wu
Ching-tzu *Wen-mu shan-fang chi* wai yi-wen ti fa-hsien" ("The Discovery of an Extant Composition Not Included in Wu Ching-tzu's *Wen-mu
shan-fang chi*"), "Wen-hsüeh yi-ch'an," *Kuang-ming jih-pao* 160 (June
9, 1957), p. 4. The Ho Tse-han reprint differs from the version in
Ch'en's article in several important places. My opinion is that the
version in Ho makes more sense and is more reliable since it is
gotten directly from Chiang Yü's work rather than copied from a second-
hand entry in a collectanea.
"Yü-ch'ao shih-ts'ao hsü" ("Preface to *Poetic Grass in a Nest of Jade*"). A
piece of parallel prose *(p'ien-wen)* attached to a collection of poems by
Hsü Tzu-chih. Reported in Pien Hsiao-hsüan, "Fa-hsien yi-p'ien Wu
Ching-tzu ti p'ien-wen" ("Discovering a Piece of Parallel Prose of Wu
Ching-tzu"), "Wen-hsüeh yi-ch'an," *Kuang-ming jih-pao* 375 (August
6, 1961), p. 4.
Ju-lin wai-shih (Unofficial History of the Literati). See Appendix.

3. Translations of the *Ju-lin wai-shih* (listed under the names of the translators).

CHANG, H. C. "Young Master Bountiful." In *Chinese Literature: Popular Fiction and Drama*. Edinburgh: Edinburgh University Press, 1973. Pp. 329–81. Includes an excellent introduction to Wu Ching-tzu and his novel and a vivid translation of chapters 31 and 32.

HSU CHEN-P'ING. "Four Eccentrics: The Epilogue to *Ju Lin Wai Shih*." *T'ien-hsia Monthly* 2, no. 2 (1940), 178–92. An early rendering of chapter 55.

YANG HSIEN-YI, and YANG, GLADYS. *The Scholars*. Peking: Foreign Languages Press, 1957. A fine, reliable and nearly complete translation. Some minor parts involving puns or unpleasant descriptions (of incidents involving excrement, for example) are left out. The disputed chapter 56 is also not included.

———, and ———. *The Scholars*. New York Grosset and Dunlap, 1972. An American reprint of the Yangs' translation; discards the original introduction by Wu Tsu-hsiang and substitutes one by C. T. Hsia. Pagination also differs from the original by thirty pages.

———, and ———. "Fan Chin passes his examinations. An excerpt from 'The Scholars.' " *People's China* 3 (February 1, 1955), 26–30. A reprint of part of chapter 3 of the *Scholars*.

———, and ———. "The Lives of the Scholars." *Chinese Literature* 4 (1954), 5–68. Excerpts of the Yangs' translation of chapters 1–7, with no mention of the translators.

SECONDARY SOURCES

CHANG CHUNG-LI. *The Chinese Gentry: Studies on Their Role in Nineteenth-Century Chinese Society*. Seattle: University of Washington Press, 1967. Uneven but useful reference work on the Chinese civil service examination system and the gentry-official system it spawned.

CHANG HUI-CHIEN. "Ju-lin wai-shih chi-ch'i tso-che" ("The *Ju-lin wai-shih* and Its Author"). In *Ju-lin wai-shih yen-chiu lün-chi*, pp. 130–39. Representative expression of the Marxist interpretation of Wu Ching-tzu's life and work.

———. "Wu Ching-tzu chiao-yu k'ao" ("A Study of Wu Ching-tzu's Acquaintances"). In *Ming-Ch'ing hsiao-shuo yen-chiu lün-wen chi* pp. 350–63. Interesting and sometimes useful bits of information on Wu's social circle.

CHANG WEN-HU (T'ien-mu shan ch'iao). *Ju-lin wai-shih p'ing (Commentary on the "Ju-lin wai-shih")*. 2 vols. Pao-wen ko (Precious Literature Alcove), 1885. Earliest extensive commentary on the *Ju-lin wai-shih*, by a Ch'ing dynasty aficionado.

CHOU SHU-JEN (Lu Hsün). *A Brief History of Chinese Fiction*. Translated by Yang Hsien-yi and Gladys Yang. 2d ed. Peking: Foreign Languages

Press, 1964. Originally published as *Chung-kuo hsiao shuo shih-lüeh* (rev. ed.) in 1930, this work is still widely quoted. Particularly interesting is the evaluation of the *Ju-lin wai-shih* (pp. 288–97) by the author, who is himself a satirist of uncommon skill.

CH'Ü T'UNG-TSU. *Local Government in China Under the Ch'ing.* Stanford: Stanford University Press, 1969. Excellent reference work for determining the duties of various local officials in Ch'ing dynasty China.

Ch'üan-chiao hsien-chih (Local Gazetteer of Ch'üan-chiao). Edited by Chang Ch'i-chün, et al. Published in 1920, in 8 *ts'e* containing 16 *chüan.* Used as a source of information on Wu Ching-tzu. The biography of Wu that it contains, however, is brief and probably copied from Ch'eng Chin-fang's "Wen-mu hsien-sheng chuan" ("Biography of Master Wen-mu").

Chūgoku no hachi dai shōsetsu (The Eight Great Novels of China), Edited by Ōsaka shiritsu daigaku Chūgoku bungaku kenkyū-shitsu (Chinese Literature Department of Osaka City College). Tokyo: Heibonsha, 1965. A misnamed (two of the eight "novels" are really collections of short stories) but useful work which includes five articles on the *Ju-lin wai-shih* by some of Japan's leading scholars on the subject.

COLEMAN, JOHN D. "With and Without a Compass: *The Scholars, The Travels of Lao Ts'an,* and the Waning of Confucian Tradition During the Ch'ing Dynasty." *Tamkang Review* 7, no. 2 (October, 1976), 61–79. A stimulating, if incomplete, discussion of the moral basis of the *Ju-lin wai-shih* in contrast to that of a well-known late Ch'ing novel.

DRYDEN, JOHN. "Discourse Concerning the Original and Progress of Satire." In *Essays of John Dryden,* edited by W. P. Ker, II, 15–114. Oxford: Oxford University Press, 1900. Despite a certain looseness of organization, this essay is a milestone in the criticism of satire. Written in 1692, many of the points it makes are still valuable to a modern critic.

ELLIOTT, ROBERT C. *The Power of Satire: Magic, Ritual, Art.* Princeton: Princeton University Press, 1960. A most important work, which traces the connections of satirical art to primitive rituals and curses.

FRYE, NORTHRUP. *Anatomy of Criticism: Four Essays.* Princeton: Princeton University Press, 1957. The insightful section on satire (pp. 223–39) has been highly influential.

GIBBS, DONALD A. "Notes on the Wind: The Term 'Feng' in Chinese Literary Criticism." In *Transition and Permanence: Chinese History and Culture.* Hong Kong: Cathay Press, 1972. Pp. 285–293. An etymological study which sheds light also on the origins of satire in Chinese letters.

HANAN, PATRICK D. "The Early Chinese Short Story: A Critical Theory in Outline." *Harvard Journal of Asiatic Studies* 27 (1967), 168–207. An interesting attempt at defining the early (before 1550) Chinese vernacular short story as a genre.

HIGHET, GILBERT. *The Anatomy of Satire.* Princeton: Princeton University Press, 1962. A highly readable and informative discussion of satire in the West, written from a series of lectures.

HO CH' I-FANG. "Wu Ching-tzu's *Scholars.*" *People's China* 3 (February 1, 1955), 17–20, 25. One of only two English language articles on the *Ju-lin wai-shih* from the People's Republic of China. Useful for those interested in a Marxist statement of the subject.

HO MAN-TZU. *Lün Ju-lin wai-shih (Discussing the "Ju-lin wai-shih").* Shanghai: Shang-hai ch'u-pan kung-ssu, 1955. A brief monograph (77 pp.) praising Wu Ching-tzu as a writer "for the people" and one who "paints a complete, realistic picture of the upper classes of his times." A generally Marxist interpretation, though Ho was later attacked as a "rightist" for this work.

HO TSE-HAN. *Ju-lin wai-shih jen-wu pen-shih k'ao-lüeh (Brief Examination of Facts Behind the Characters of the "Ju-lin wai-shih").* Shanghai: Ku-tien wen-hsüeh ch'u-pan she, 1957. Undoubtedly the most important and indispensible single work for the researcher. Especially valuable are the reprints of the most important primary source materials: biographies of Wu Ching-tzu by Ch'eng Chin-fang ("Wen-mu hsien-sheng chuan") and Chin Ho (the unabridged version of his postscript) as well as biographical poems by Wu's relatives and acquaintances, some hitherto unknown.

HSIA, C. T. *The Classic Chinese Novel.* New York: Columbia University Press, 1968. A superbly written introduction to the six major novels of traditional China. The *Ju-lin wai-shih* is discussed in Chapter 6, pp. 203–44.

HU SHIH. "Wu Ching-tzu chuan" ("Biography of Wu Ching-tzu"). In *Hu Shih wen-ts'un (Collected Works of Hu Shih).* Shanghai: Ya-tung t'u-shu kuan, 1921–1940. Vol. 1, *chüan* 4, pp. 225–35. First modern biography of Wu Ching-tzu, written in 1920. Ch'eng Chin-fang's important biography and poem concerning Wu are included in an appendix.

———. "Wu Ching-tzu nien-p'u" ("Chronology of Wu Ching-tzu's Life"). In *Hu Shih wen-ts'un.* Vol. 2 *chüan* 4, pp. 1–50. A new biography, completed in 1922, and including for the first time the four-*chüan* *Wen-mu shan-fang chi* as a source. Much of this pioneering study is still valid and useful.

HUMMEL, ARTHUR W., ed. *Eminent Chinese of the Ch'ing Period.* Washington, D.C.: U.S. Government Printing Office, 1943–1944. Vol. 2, pp. 866–67. The biography of Wu Ching-tzu is by Tu Lien-che and is a convenient, if somewhat dated, reference.

IIDA YOSHIRŌ. "Jurin gaishi no kinkyū to shiryō" ("Studies and Materials

Concerning the *Ju-lin wai-shih*"). *Chugoku no hachi dai shosetsu*,
pp. 309–18. A useful though incomplete summary of the texts of the
novel, as well as important Japanese studies on it.
INADA TAKASHI. "Jurin gaishi no iwayuru kōteiteki jimbutsu ni tsuite"
("Concerning the So-called Positive Characters of the *Ju-lin wai-shih*").
*Tōkyō Gakugei Daigaku kenkyū hōkoku (Research Reports of the
Tokyo University of Arts and Sciences)* 13, no. 11 (1962), 21–29. An
important and stimulating discussion of the moral bases of the *Ju-lin
wai-shih* by its Japanese translator.
Ju-lin wai-shih yen-chiu lün-chi (Collection of Research Articles on the Ju-lin
wai-shih). Edited by Tso-chia ch'u-pan she. Peking: Tso-chia ch'u-pan
she, 1955. A collection of studies by some of the most prominent
scholars in the People's Republic of China. A basic work for anyone
interested in the Marxist interpretation.
KAO YU-KUNG. "Lyrical Vision in Chinese Narrative Tradition: A Reading of
Hung-lou meng and *Ju-lin wai-shih.*" In *Chinese Narrative: Critical
and Theoretical Essays*, edited by Andrew H. Plaks, pp. 227–43.
Princeton: Princeton University Press, 1977. A learned discussion of
the classical nature of the two greatest novels of the Ch'ing period.
KAWANO MASAAKI. "Jurin gaishi kō" ("A Study of the *Ju-lin wai-shih*"). *Kan
bungaku (Chinese Literature)* 11 August, 1964), 19–25. Contains useful information on the texts of the novel; should be used with the article
by Iida and the *Catalogue* of Sun K'ai-ti.
KERNAN, ALVIN B. *The Plot of Satire*. New Haven: Yale University Press,
1965. A highly insightful work on the satirical plot. Its pervasive
influence on this study is obvious.
KRÁL, OLDŘICH. "Several Artistic Methods in the Classic Chinese Novel
Ju-lin wai-shih." *Archiv Orientalni* 32 (January, 1964), 16–43. For a
long time, the only in-depth study of the *Ju-lin wai-shih* by a
Westerner. It examines the novel not as satire, but as a work of
realism.
LEVENSON, JOSEPH R. "The Amateur Ideal in Ming and Early Ch'ing Society: Evidence from Painting." In *Confucian China and Its Modern
Fate: A Trilogy*. Berkeley: University of California Press, 1968.
Pp. 15–43. The findings in this article are highly relevant to the ques-
tion of the positive morality in the *Ju-lin wai-shih*.
LI CHU-TSING. "Problems Concerning the Life of Wang Mien, Painter of
Plum Blossoms." *Renditions*, no. 6 (Spring, 1976), 111–123. An excel-
lent summary of the various versions of Wang Mien's biography, in-
cluding the highly fictionalized one in the *Ju-lin wai-shih*.
LIN SHUEN-FU. "Ritual and Narrative Structure in *Ju-lin Wai-shih.*" In
Chinese Narrative: Critical and Theoretical Essays, pp. 244–65. An
attempt to analyze the structure of the *Ju-lin wai-shih* in terms of the

philosophical underpinnings of Chinese culture rather than of the satirical nature of the work itself.

LIU TA-CHIEH. "Ju-lin wai-shih yü feng-tz'u wen hsüeh" ("The *Ju-lin wai-shih* and Satirical Literature"). In *Ju-lin wai-shih yen-chiu lün-chi*, pp. 82–91. A brief article by an eminent literary historian on the importance of the *Ju-lin wai-shih;* includes commentary on the novel's portrayal of women.

LIU TS'UN-YAN. *Chinese Popular Fiction in Two London Libraries.* Hong Kong: Lung Men Bookstore, 1967. Contains a good discussion of textual problems of the *Ju-lin wai-shih.*

Ming-Ch'ing hsiao-shuo yen chiu lün-wen chi (Collection of Research Studies of Ming and Ch'ing Fiction). Edited by Jen-min wen-hsüeh ch'u-pan she pien-chi pu (editorial section). Peking: Jen-min wen-hsüeh ch'u-pan she, 1959. Includes important articles on the *Ju-lin wai-shih* and its author.

MOTE FREDERICK W. "Confucian Eremitism in the Yüan Period." In *Confucianism and Chinese Civilization*, edited by Arthur F. Wright, pp. 252–90. New York: Atheneum, 1965. An illuminating study of a lesser-known aspect of Confucianism which helps to account for the behavior of the exemplary characters in the *Ju-lin wai-shih.*

NIVISON, DAVID S. "Protest Against Conventions and Conventions of Protest." In *Confucianism and Chinese Civilization*, pp. 227–51. Reveals the tension between the idealistic and practical sides of Confucianism throughout Chinese history. Along with Mote's article above, it illuminates the moral message in the *Ju-lin wai-shih.*

OGAWA TAMAKI, "Jurin gaishi no keishiki to naiyō" ("The Form and Content of the *Ju-lin wai-shih*"). In *Chūgoku shōsetsu-shi no kenkyū (Studies in the History of Chinese Fiction).* Tokyo: Iwanami shoten, 1968. Pp. 181–97. Written in 1933, this article is a genuine pioneering work which, even now, appears full of provocative and valuable insights.

ROPP, PAUL STANLEY. "Early Ch'ing Society and Its Critics: The Life and Times of Wu Ching-tzu (1701–1754)." Ph.D. dissertation, University of Michigan, 1974. An historian's view of Wu and his novel, interesting as comparison to this study, with which it differs in both focus and a number of conclusions.

SHEN YEN-PING (Mao Tun). "Wu Ching-tzu hsien-sheng shih-shih erh-pai chou-nien chi-nien k'ai-mu tz'u" ("Opening Address for the Commemoration of the Bicentennial of Mr. Wu Ching-tzu's Death"). *Kuang-ming jih-pao* 33 (December 12, 1954), p. 4. A brief speech by the then minister of culture of the People's Republic of China. Important because it sets the tone and direction for nearly all subsequent Chinese Marxist articles on the *Ju-lin wai-shih* and its author.

SUN K'AI-TI. *Chung-kuo t'ung-su hsiao-shuo shu-mu (Catalogue of Popular*

Chinese Fiction). Rev. ed. Hong Kong: Shih-yung shu-chü, 1967. The standard reference work for textual information on works of Chinese fiction.

WANG WEI-LIN. "Ts'ung liang-pu shih-ch-li so chien-tao ti yu-kuan Wu Ching-tzu ti tzu-liao" ("Material Concerning Wu Ching-tzu Seen in Two Collections of Poetry"). In *Wen-hsüeh yi-ch'an tseng-k'an (A Supplement to the Literary Heritage Series)*. Peking: Chung-hua shu-chü, 1962. Vol. 11, pp. 166–76. An extremely valuable source for facts on Wu Ching-tzu's personal life: his places of residence, his marriages, his offspring, and his death. The collections consulted are those of his friend Wu P'ei-yüan and his son Wu Lang.

WELLS, HENRY W. "An Essay on the *Ju-Lin Wai-Shih*." *Tamkang Review* 2, no. 1 (April, 1971), 143–52. As good a statement as any on the problem of interpretation which the *Ju-lin wai-shih* presents to the modern scholar.

WU TSU-HSIANG. " 'Ju-lin wai-shih' ti ssu-hsiang ho yi-shu" ("The Thought and Art of the *Ju-lin wai-shih*"). In *Ju-lin wai-shih yen-chiu lün-chi*, pp. 1–38. The only article to clearly point out Wu Ching-tzu's debt to traditional Chinese historiography.

———. "The Realism of Wu Ching-tzu." *Chinese Literature* 4 (April, 1954), 155–65. Included in the original edition of *The Scholars* as an introduction; restates some of the basic Marxist tenets concerning the novel.

Index

(Except for certain individual poems and lyrics which supply biographical information and are listed separately, the works of Wu Ching-tzu are listed under his name)